How to Say It® to Your Dog

Most Prentice Hall Press books are available at special quantity discounts for bulk purchases for sales promotions, premiums, fund-raising, or educational use. Special books, or book excerpts, can also be created to fit specific needs.

For details, write: Special Markets, Penguin Group (USA) Inc., 375 Hudson Street, New York, New York 10014.

How to Say It® to Your Dog

Solving

Behavior Problems

in Ways Your Dog Will Understand

JANINE ADAMS

The health-related information in the book is not intended as medical advice. Its intent is informational and educational. Please consult a veterinarian should the need for one be indicated.

Published by The Berkley Publishing Group
A member of Penguin Group (USA) Inc.
375 Hudson Street
New York, New York 10014

Text design by Tiffany Estreicher
Cover design by Charles Björklund

Prentice Hall Press edition: November 2003

ISBN: 0-7352-0350-4

This book has been cataloged by the Library of Congress

Printed in the United States of America

10 9 8 7 6 5 4 3 2 1

This book is dedicated to the memory of Kramer and Scout, much-loved Standard Poodles, who got me started as a dog writer. They are missed every day.

Contents

part three
Communicating Through Training 85

part four
A Positive Approach to Specific Behavior Challenges 105

Acknowledgments

I wish to thank the positive trainers of the world, who lead by example and do so much for the welfare and happiness of dogs and their people.

Thank you to Michael Snell, my agent, for bringing this project to me. Thanks also to Tom Power, senior editor at Prentice Hall, who was pleasantly responsive and encouraging as I prepared the manuscript. And to Michelle Howry, Perigee Books editor, who is a joy to work with.

Thanks to Shannon Wilkinson, for input on TTouch and for listening to me kvetch; to Sally Brown, for her marvelous contribution and support; and to a special group of Internet friends: Gina Barnett, Ann Daugherty, Amy Heggie, and Susan Lennon, whose perspective on dogs (and life) I appreciate so much.

And finally, a big thank you to my husband, Barry Marcus, who supports me in everything I do. And to Pip, our new Poodle, who has already taught me so much.

Introduction

Canine Communication and What It Means to You and Your Dog

Dogs might not speak English (or any other human language), but they are consummate communicators. Dogs read the subtlest shifts in body language and intonation. They're exquisitely sensitive to nonverbal communication. We humans, on the other hand, focus so much on words that our perceptions of other forms of communication are dulled.

If we learn to pay more attention to what our dogs are telling us—and to what we're telling our dogs—we can live in harmony and happiness with our canine friends. We're communicating in every interaction we have with dogs. Unfortunately, much of the time, that communication is negative. Have you ever joked that your dog thinks his name is "No"? Traditional, correction-based techniques of training and problem-solving in which dogs are corrected more than they're rewarded can be damaging to the dog-human relationship. Positive training techniques, on the other hand, can enhance the relationship and help make problem behaviors disappear.

This book is intended to help make life with your dog more peaceful and enjoyable. It suggests positive strategies for dealing with behavior problems. It discourages the use of force or pain in interacting with your dog. If you embrace a positive philosophy with your dog (focusing on what you want your dog to do, not what you don't want him to do; rewarding good behavior instead of correcting undesired behavior), chances are that problem behaviors will become less prevalent. And life will become more pleasant for both you and your dog.

How We Communicate with Our Dogs

Some of our communication with dogs is out loud. We'll keep a running commentary going with our dogs whether or not we believe they can actually understand us. (I think many dogs understand much more language than most people give them credit for.) But we also communicate through our eyes and with our bodies, tone of voice, and touch. We even communicate telepathically.

Our dogs are communicating right back. They use vocalizations (how many of your dog's different barks can you recognize?), body language, calming signals, and touch to communicate with other dogs and with us. Every dog lover knows that dogs smile and wag their tails to express pleasure (although a wagging tail can express other emotions as well). Getting to know your dog's modes of communication will open new levels of understanding between the two of you.

So you're talking with your dog and he's talking right back, yet there's still plenty of miscommunication! Why is that? Perhaps you're sending mixed signals to your dog. Or maybe you're not interpreting his attempts to communicate with you accurately. Learning about how dogs communicate with one another will help you figure out how your dog is communicating with you. And you can even use some of those communication techniques with your dog.

BODY LANGUAGE

Dogs have many ways of communicating, most of them silent. Body language is a very important means of communication for dogs; once you learn the basics of canine body language, you'll be able to recognize what your dog is communicating to other dogs and to you.

The best way to learn your dog's body language is to watch him interacting with other dogs, preferably off-leash, because leashes can restrict your dog's vocabulary. If you have access to a dog park, you're in luck. It's a regular laboratory for observing and learning about canine communication. Once you can spot your dog's body language, you'll be able to notice when your dog is using it with you. And if you're really savvy, you'll be able to start using some canine-based body language with your dog!

You can learn to understand whether your dog is feeling friendly or aggressive, relaxed or afraid, submissive or dominant by keeping an eye on the various body parts he uses to communicate. The following tables summarize these signals.

Much of this information is detailed—and illustrated—in *Dog Language: An Encyclopedia of Canine Behavior* by Roger Abrantes and *How to Speak Dog: Mastering the Art of Dog-Human Communication* by Stanley Coren.

Of course, it is the combination of the various body parts that creates the whole picture. For example, both submissive and friendly dogs might have narrowed eyes and might blink. But the submissive dog will also have a low, cringing posture and tucked tail, while the relaxed, friendly dog might have a more erect posture and a wagging tail.

Dogs with docked tails have a harder time using their tail as a communication tool. Many will exaggerate their movement to compensate, like the stub-tailed dogs who wag their whole hind end. Some breeds, like Terriers, have naturally upright tails, which can make them appear dominant, even if they're not.

Ear signals are most easily read on dogs with prick ears. But lop-eared or long-eared dogs also use their ears to communicate. If you look closely, you can see when a Poodle's ears are pricked. The ear messages in these dogs are much more subtle.

Context makes all the difference in interpreting body language. A dog who is eliciting play from another dog might draw his lips back and show his teeth, with ears erect, which could, in other situations, indicate aggression. But the rest of his body language—perhaps a play bow or lifting a paw in the direction of his playmate—lets you know it's all in fun. The way dogs play mimics fighting, so it's understandable that their invitations to play might mimic precursors to fighting.

Bear in mind that a dog can be submissive and aggressive at the same time.

	Friendly	Aggressive	Afraid
Eyes	Blinking, averted gaze	Wide open, staring	Narrowed, blinking
Ears	Back, relaxed	Erect	Back, flattened
Mouth	Lips back, mouth open	Bared teeth, raised lips	Lips drawn back, mouth closed
Body posture	Loose	Puffed up, straight back	Low, cringing
Head	Smooth forehead	High	Low
Tail	High (but not erect), broadly wagging	Stiff horizontal, slight wagging	Tucked
Other			Rapid breathing, sweating through pads

This happens when a submissive dog's efforts at showing submission fail and the dog can't run away. A submissive, aggressive dog will have flattened ears and tucked tail but will also show his teeth (although his lips will be drawn back rather than forward in the snarl of a dominant, aggressive dog).

CALMING SIGNALS

In addition to postures and expressions, dogs use a set of signals to calm agitated or fearful dogs. They use these signals on their people, too—and you can use them on your dog. Norwegian dog trainer and enthusiast Turid Rugaas recognized and named these signs as she observed dogs interacting with one another. She identified twenty-seven different signals, which she calls calming signals, that dogs use to avoid conflict and to maintain the peace. She describes these signals in her book *On Talking Terms with Animals: Calming Signals* and video *Calming Signals: What Your Dog Tells You.*

The calming signals include the following:

Relaxed	Dominant	Submissive
Soft	Wide open, staring	Narrowed, blinking, averted gaze
Forward	Erect	Back, flattened
Slightly open, tongue visible	Bared teeth	Lips drawn back, mouth closed
Loose	Straight back, stiff	Low, cringing, arched back
High	Raised	Low
Down but not tucked, occasional swishing	Erect	Lowered or tucked
		Raised paw, rolled on back, licking the muzzle of the other dog

- Looking away
- Turning the entire head away from the other dog (which is done when looking away doesn't do the trick)
- Yawning
- Licking lips
- Sitting and lying down or freezing in place
- Sniffing the ground
- Approaching the other dog at a curve
- Moving slowly
- Pretending to do something else

- Crouching in a play bow
- Marking
- Splitting up (that is, going between two other dogs or two people)

When you're around a pair or group of dogs, watch how they interact. If they're unfamiliar with one another, they might approach slowly and sniff the ground before they come together. If one dog is fearful or just annoying, the other dog might turn his head away or sit or lie down. Once you become familiar with the signals it's fascinating to watch.

Your dog might be using these signals on you, too! If you bellow for your dog to come, he might approach you much more slowly, in an effort to calm you, than if you called him in a happy voice. If your dog is in a stressful or scary situation, like at the vet's office, you might see her yawn.

You can turn the tables and use the calming signals on your dog (or other dogs, for that matter). If your dog is nervous about a new person, ask that person to yawn. If your dog is nervous about another dog, step between them to split them up. Your dog will understand this calming signal. If you come across a dog who is nervous about you, yawn at him, turn your head away from him, or approach him from the side rather than head-on. That might make him feel more comfortable.

TELEPATHIC COMMUNICATION

Animals and humans communicate telepathically. It sounds a little crazy when it's stated like that, but I believe it to be fact. When I was researching my book *You Can Talk to Your Animals: Animal Communicators Tell You How* (Howell Book House, 2000), I spoke with eleven professional animal communicators—people who are paid to communicate telepathically with animals—and scores of their clients. Time and time again, I heard how using the services of animal communicators benefited the animals and their people.

But everybody has the ability to communicate without words. We humans have closed off that part of our mind though, and don't take advantage of this skill that has so much potential to help us connect with and build relationships with our pets. You can easily harness the power of telepathic communication by talking aloud to your dog. Throughout this book, you will see suggestions for visualizing positive outcomes and talking aloud to your dog. If your dog is particularly verbal, he might understand the words you say to him. But behind every utterance is a telepathic message, and your dog is very likely to pick up that message.

But you can take it a step further and learn to receive the telepathic messages your dog is sending to you. See the appendix for titles of books that can help you rediscover this skill. It's simply a matter of quieting your mind, sending a message to your dog by thinking it, then opening your quiet mind for a response. Then comes the hardest part: believing that the response you receive—I can promise you that something will go through your mind—is coming from your dog. If you can get over that hurdle of trusting what you receive, you can take your relationship with your dog to a deeper level.

FLOWER REMEDIES

Throughout the book, flower remedies are suggested to help address the emotions of dogs (and owners) in various situations. Developed seventy years ago by Edward Bach, a homeopath and physician, flower remedies, also known as flower essences, use tiny amounts of plant material from specific flowers soaked in water (the flowers are then discarded) and preserved in brandy. The remedies are used to heal on an emotional/spiritual level. Specific flower remedies are used to treat specific emotional issues (like jealousy or anxiety), while various combination products, like the popular "Rescue Remedy"—a combination of five flower essences—tend to have a more general use. Several companies make flower essences, including Bach, Anaflora, and Flower Essence Services (FES). They're safe and can be quite effective.

TELLINGTON TTOUCH

A three-part bodywork system, Tellington TTouch is probably best known for the centerpiece of the system: circular touches (called TTouches) performed on an animal. The system also includes the Leading Exercises (a series of training aids) and the Confidence Course, a fun and therapeutic agility course that increases confidence, focus, and balance by having the dog work muscles in nonhabitual ways.

TTouch inventor Linda Tellington-Jones refers to TTouch as "a nonverbal language." The goal of TTouch bodywork is to stimulate the function and vitality of the animal's cells and activate unused neural pathways to the brain. In this way, TTouch helps change the animal's habitual behavior and emotions.

In addition to the behavioral and emotional benefits of TTouch, the TTouches are fun to do on your dog. They're relaxing for the dog and great for your relationship, as you gain your dog's trust and communicate your love and caring through your touch. With all these advantages, it's worthwhile to make a little effort to learn about TTouch. Tellington-Jones has written a new dog-specific TTouch book (originally developed on horses, the system works on other animals as well) called *Getting in TTouch with Your Dog: A Gentle Approach to Influencing Behavior, Health, and Performance*. She has also produced an instructional video, *Unleash Your Dog's Potential: Getting in TTouch with Your Canine Friend*. In addition, you can schedule an appointment with a TTouch practitioner, who will teach you in person how to do TTouch on your dog.

The very basic component of the system is the Clouded Leopard circular touch. The other circular touches are variations on the Clouded Leopard. With this touch, you make light circles with your finger pads on the dog's body. Moving just the skin, you start at 6 o'clock, go all the way around and end at 8 or 9. You then move to another spot and do another circle. You can keep going until you or your dog is tired of it. (Never force TTouch on your dog—if he walks away, let him. But be prepared for him to come back for more.)

The other important TTouch doesn't include a circular motion. The Ear TTouch calms and soothes frightened or hyperactive dogs. With the Ear TTouch, you stroke the dog's ear from the base to the tip, using a gentle, horizontal stroke (except on dogs with prick ears, in which case you should use an upward motion). Put the ear between your thumb and forefinger (with your thumb on top of the ear) and gently stroke. Make sure you cover every inch of the dog's ear. You should hold out the ears of long-eared dogs (like Poodles and Cocker Spaniels) so they're horizontal to the floor. If the ear is very large, support it on one hand while you stroke it with the other. The Ear TTouch also helps dogs who have suffered trauma or who are going into shock. In those cases, perform the Ear TTouch—with a firm touch and quick stroke—on the way to the vet's office.

Training: The Positive Way to Communicate with Your Dog

The idea of training a dog once conjured up images of boring, repetitive tasks that dog and owner had to practice during eight weeks of training class. Those training sessions might involve yanking the dog around or speaking very sternly whenever the dog didn't do what was asked of him. For many dog owners, it was a necessary but unenjoyable aspect of dog ownership.

But people who train their puppies and dogs using positive methods know differently. They've learned that training is a fun and productive way to spend quality time with your dog while teaching him how you want him to behave.

Positive-reinforcement-based training techniques go beyond "training sessions." They influence the way you interact with your dog, your understanding of his motivations, even the way you think about your dog.

Traditional training methods tend to pit people against dogs. The prevailing theory was that dogs were essentially wolves who hung out with people, and the best way to treat a dog was to pretend you're a wolf. And you'd better be the alpha wolf or your dog would try to take over. Proponents of this theory suggested that dogs who were acting "dominant" toward their people should be forcibly put on their backs in an "alpha roll" that was supposed to replicate the way wolves physically dominate one another.

But the alpha roll isn't easy for most owners to do. It is unpleasant for dog and owner, and it is dangerous—with the human's face so close to the dog's, any dog who is inclined to bite (as a dog in need of an alpha roll might be) has every opportunity to do so.

The alpha roll comes part and parcel with the negative, physical nature of traditional, correction-based training. These methods rely on telling the dog what to do (never mind that he doesn't yet know what the words mean), then physically forcing him to do it and correcting him (sometimes harshly) if he strays from the request.

Luckily for dogs and their humans, the times are changing. A different way to look at dogs, to interact with them, and to train them is becoming increasingly popular. Positive-reinforcement-based training recognizes that dogs are not motivated to please their humans. They're motivated to please themselves. Traditional training works because the dog wants to please himself by avoiding punishment. Positive training works because the dog is rewarded for doing the right thing. And when he does something that isn't what the human wants, he's simply not rewarded. But he's not corrected, either. The interaction between human and dog remains positive.

This type of training is based on the principle that behavior that is reinforced tends to be repeated. In positive training, desirable behaviors are reinforced; undesirable behaviors are ignored. It is the basis for the problem-solving techniques found in this book. It's humane, it's fun, and it builds your bond with your dog (rather than potentially making your dog fear you). Best of all, it works.

When you decide to start training your dog, I strongly urge you to seek out a positive trainer. It might take a little effort to find one and it might (or might not) even cost a little more money, but it's worth it, because it will help strengthen your relationship with your dog while making him an even better companion than he was before.

WHEN CAN YOU START TRAINING?

The once-commonplace notion that dogs shouldn't attend a training class until they're six months old is based on the traditional, correction-based training, which relied on jerks on the chain collar, as well as physically placing dogs into desired positions. Puppy necks are too delicate to be jerked around, and pups who are handled roughly can become hand-shy.

But positive training, using lures and/or clicks (see below) and lots of treats, can—and should—start the moment a puppy enters your life. By starting a positive training program when the pup is very young, he learns that human hands bring only good things.

A dog of any age can be trained. If your dog is already an adolescent or adult (or even a senior citizen!) you can start working with him today, using positive methods, to modify any undesired behaviors and to teach him some fun skills.

CLICKER TRAINING

Timing is important in positive training. You want your dog to know what behavior you are reinforcing. But it can be hard to deliver a treat at precisely the right time. If you pair the treat with a clicker (a small plastic box with a flexible piece of metal inside that makes a distinctive "click" when pressed), you're able to provide precise information to your dog about what behavior is being rewarded.

The power of the clicker is immense. It must be paired with a treat (food, play, or some other reward) in order to have any meaning. A click isn't effective without a treat. Dogs (or other animals, for that matter) catch on quickly that click = treat. They know that whatever it is they're doing when they hear the click is what they're being rewarded for.

Because of the power of the clicker, I've chosen to use instructions to click and treat throughout this book. Some people resist using a clicker, saying that they're too uncoordinated or they don't always have a clicker handy. Those people can use a tongue cluck or what trainers call a bridge word instead of a click. For example, they can say "Good!" or "Yes!" in place of clicking the clicker. This approach has a major drawback, however: A verbal cue is not as precise as a click. It's harder to be accurate in your timing when using a bridge word or a tongue cluck. On the other hand, the bridge word or tongue cluck is always with you. If you prefer not to use a clicker (although I strongly encourage you to buy a clicker, read a clicker-training book, and try it out—I think you'll be amazed at the difference a clicker makes), you can substitute your bridge word whenever this book says to click your dog.

Remember, whether you're using a click, a tongue cluck, or a bridge word, you must do two things: First, you must teach your dog that click = treat by clicking and treating a few times in a row, until your dog perks up whenever he hears a click (or tongue cluck or bridge word) and looks to you for a treat. (Clicker trainers call this "charging the clicker.") Second, you must *always* follow the click with a treat.

Dominance Versus Leadership

As mentioned earlier, common wisdom long held that it's important that you be dominant over your dog. But that theory of human/dog dominance—and the underlying assumption that a dog will try to be dominant over the human when given the opportunity—is starting to be questioned by modern trainers and behaviorists.

The problem with labeling a dog as "dominant" and taking steps to assert human dominance over the dog is that people are often advised to use physical means to show their dogs who's boss. Scruff shakes (in which the human grabs the fur on either side of a dog's face and shakes the dog's head) and alpha rolls are supposed to mimic alpha wolf behavior (a fallacy, it has been pointed out, because alpha wolves rarely have to exert their dominance). The problem with these physical methods is that (a) they're dangerous to the human, who puts herself at risk of being bitten in the face, (b) they scare the dog, and (c) they're damaging to the human/dog relationship.

Instead, most positive trainers point to a model of leadership—benevolent leadership, that is. You don't have to physically accost your dog. You don't have to be vigilant about making sure that you always eat first, that you precede your dog out the door, or that your dog never gets on the furniture or sleeps in your bed. Positive trainers point out that dogs do what is rewarding to them. Behaviors that were once viewed as "dominant" (rushing to go out the door first, resisting being hauled off the bed, etc.) are simply behaviors that the dog finds rewarding (he wants to get outside; the bed is comfy; and it's scary to be manhandled).

If you're faced with a dog who is a natural-born leader and you fear that he is challenging your leadership, don't take it upon yourself to physically dominate your dog. Instead, act like a benevolent leader and reinforce the notion that you provide the things your dog wants and that you do so under your terms.

One way to do this is through what some call a "Nothing in Life Is Free" program. It's fairly simple: The dog learns to look to you to get things he values and he has to earn those things. For example, if you ask for a sit before giving your dog a treat or letting him in the yard or feeding him his supper, you will soon have a dog who sits readily. Looked at through human eyes, sitting is a very polite behavior. Your dog might sit to ask you to give him a treat, and you might (or might not) choose to reward that sit. Isn't it more pleasant if your dog asks for a treat by sitting rather than pawing you or barking at you? There's no doubt about it: A Nothing in Life Is Free program is certainly more pleasant for human and dog than a series of alpha rolls—and it's equally effective, if not more.

There's no need to institute a Nothing in Life Is Free policy with your dog if you aren't experiencing leadership issues. But if you are experiencing some behavior problems that you think would benefit from your being a stronger leader in your dog's eyes, it's easy to institute and implement the Nothing in Life Is Free program. There's a chapter in this book called "Leadership Issues" that provides more information on how you can exert yourself as your dog's benevolent leader.

Positive trainers find that "dominance" or leadership issues don't tend to come up when people use positive reinforcement as the basis for treating their dogs. If the dog is rewarded for doing what the human wants, and ignored for doing anything else, he'll repeat the desired behaviors. Sure, he's doing it to please himself, rather than the human, but who cares?

A Word About the Word *Punishment*

In scientific terms, punishment is something that reduces the likelihood of a behavior being repeated. It can be positive punishment—that is, adding something to make a behavior stop (for example, kneeing a dog in the chest when he jumps on you)—or negative punishment—taking something away to make a behavior stop (withdrawing your attention by turning your back on a dog who is jumping on you).

The flip side of the coin is reinforcement, or anything that increases the likelihood that a behavior will be repeated. It, too, can be positive and negative: Positive reinforcement means adding something to get a behavior repeated. For example, giving a dog a treat when he sits. Negative reinforcement is taking something away in order to get a behavior repeated. A choke chain is a good example of negative reinforcement: The dog is pulling and the chain is strangling him. When he stops pulling, the choking stops. Thus, not pulling is reinforced.

In this book, I advocate humane methods of treating your dog and addressing behavior problems. That involves the use of positive reinforcement, but it also involves the use of negative punishment, like withdrawing attention or giving your dog a time-out. In operant-conditioning terms, the methods I do *not* recommend are positive punishment and negative reinforcement.

All that said, throughout the body of the book, I use the word *punishment* to mean positive punishment (and sometimes negative reinforcement). Because I assume people will refer to individual chapters rather than reading this book cover to cover, I think it's best to use the word as it is understood by the general reader. So although technically I do recommend some solutions that employ (negative) punishment, when I write, "Don't punish your dog," I'm saying, "Don't use positive punishment."

part one

General Care of Your Dog

Caring for your dog is a lot more than providing food and shelter. Dogs require, at the very minimum, companionship, exercise, veterinary care, and love. If you want to maximize your enjoyment of your dog, you'll develop a true relationship with her. To do that, you need to spend time with your dog, focus on her needs, listen to what your dog is trying to tell you, and appreciate your dog for the thinking, sentient being she is.

Make your dog a full-fledged member of the family. Be patient with her and give her the benefit of the doubt, like you would any other family member. Focus on the positive and try to just ignore the negative. You'll reap huge benefits from embracing your dog as an individual and letting her become a big part of your life.

chapter one

Adding a Second Dog

Leo and Sandy were afraid that their beloved Pug, Milo, was lonely during the day when they were at work. Milo got along well with other dogs and enjoyed having canine friends come over for visits, so the couple thought about adding another dog to the family. But things were going so well with Milo, they were afraid of upsetting the apple cart. What if Milo didn't like the new dog? Or what if the new dog diminished, rather than enhanced, his life?

Adding a second dog can be a wonderful thing for the dog you already have, and it can be great fun for you, too. But it's not right for every situation. Before you rush to add a dog to your family, give some thought to your motivations, how you'll handle the day-to-day aspects of life with more than one dog, and how your existing dog will feel about it. It's a decision not to be entered into lightly.

WHAT YOUR DOG IS TRYING TO TELL YOU

- *"I'd like a new brother or sister."* If your dog is well behaved and highly sociable, he might well benefit from a new canine family member.

- *"Why on earth would I want another dog?"* If your dog doesn't tend to enjoy the company of other dogs or is very old or infirm, adding a dog might make your dog miserable.

- *"Let's double the trouble."* If your dog's a hellion with a lot of excess energy, what she might need is more time with you, not with another dog. If you find that you don't have time to properly care for your existing dog, you're asking for trouble by adding another dog to your care. Your troublemaker might teach the new dog all her bad habits and then you'd have twice the problem!

HOW TO SAY IT

- *Do some trial runs.* Try taking care of one of your dog's friends for a weekend or a week. (As a side benefit, it's a great way to get someone to care for your dog when you're on vacation!) While you're caring for the new dog, observe how your dog handles having to share you. And take note of how easy or difficult it is for you to care for the extra dog. Two dogs are often more than twice the work of one!

- *Add a dog for the right reasons.* Do you have extra love to spare? Plenty of time and money? A dog who enjoys canine companionship? These are good reasons to add a dog.

- *Consider the implications.* Before you add another dog to your family, make sure you can afford it. You'll double your food, boarding, and grooming expenses, and you'll certainly have higher veterinary bills.

- *Make sure your existing dog is well behaved and housetrained before adding a dog.* You don't want him teaching bad habits to the new dog!

- *Familiarize yourself with calming signals before you add a dog.* That way, when the newcomer joins your family, you can watch for these signs when the two interact. It'll give you insight into how each is feeling and how they feel about one another.

- *Select the second dog carefully.* Ask yourself whether you would be better off with a puppy or an adult dog. Same breed or different? Same gender as your dog or the opposite? Provided your dogs are neutered, most experts recommend getting dogs of the opposite sex to maintain maximum peace in your household.

- *Be prepared.* When you add a dog, make sure each dog has his own food and water bowls, leash, and collar, as well as toys, bed, and crate. Put away all toys before the new dog comes home so they'll have nothing around to quarrel over.

- *Introduce the dogs carefully.* If you can, introduce the dogs on neutral ground. Ideally, that will be in a securely fenced area so your resident dog can be off-leash or dragging a leash. If you're tense about the meeting, you'll only make your dog more tense by holding the leash tight. Your dog will be more comfortable if he can get away from the newcomer.

- *Stay upbeat.* Let the dogs sniff and get to know one another. If they hit it off and you're in a safe area, perhaps they can play for a little while. Then walk them home together.

- *After you get home, be alert.* Supervise the dogs when they're together. Watch for any signs of tension and separate them (this is where crates come in handy) if tempers start to flare. If you have to leave them alone at the beginning, keep them separated.

- *Feed the dogs separately.* Don't put your dogs in a position where they'll be prompted to fight.

HOW NOT TO SAY IT

- *Don't add a dog out of guilt.* If you're feeling guilty about not spending enough time with your dog, don't add a dog to try to alleviate your dog's boredom. Instead, figure out a way to spend more time with your dog. If you were to add a dog, you'd still need to spend more time with your dog—and now you'll have two dogs to care for.

- *Don't add a dog as a substitute for exercise.* Your dog needs proper exercise, outside your yard. He needs to spend quality time with you getting that exercise. Don't fool yourself into thinking that adding a playmate will rid you of the responsibility of giving your dogs sufficient exercise!

- *Don't burden an elderly or ill dog with a canine companion.* If your dog is quite old or infirm, a new dog might just make him crabby and unhappy. If he's not able to play, being pestered by the new dog won't be any fun.
- *Don't shower all your attention on the new dog.* Be sure your first dog isn't neglected as you get to know the new one.

chapter two

Adopting an Adult Dog

When Antonia adopted her Lab mix, Zoey, at the local shelter, she was delighted to give a needy older dog a loving home. But she was a little nervous about how this six-year-old dog would adapt to her home and family. Should she treat Zoey any differently than she would a puppy? Would Zoey have issues from past experiences that Antonia should be aware of?

Adopting an adult dog can be a wonderful thing. Most adults are much less trouble than little puppies. They're often already housetrained and have outgrown obnoxious puppy behaviors. Bringing home an adult dog isn't much different than preparing your house for the arrival of a puppy, but the experience might well be easier.

WHAT YOUR DOG IS TRYING TO TELL YOU

- *"What's going on?"* If your new dog has been shuffled from place to place (even if it's just from his original home to the shelter to you), arriving at your home might be confusing.

- *"I don't know the rules."* You'll need to teach your dog, with patience, what you expect of her. If you don't know what the rules were in her former home, you don't know what she considers acceptable behavior.

- *"I'm afraid."* If your new dog isn't a confident dog, the uncertainty of the situation he finds himself in might be enough to trigger fears. He might shy away from your touch or even growl to keep you from touching him. This isn't necessarily an indication of things to come.

HOW TO SAY IT

- *Talk to your dog.* Sit down with your new dog and quietly tell him what's going on. Let him know that he's found his new home and that you will always be kind to him. Your tone will no doubt comfort him, and he may well understand your words.

- *Be patient and fair.* Try to put yourself in your dog's place. You might not know her past. You probably don't know how she handles change. Take it easy, be there for her, and don't expect her to be perfect.

- *Set limits.* Your dog will need you to show him the rules of house. Set limits for him and be consistent in enforcing those limits. This will help your dog feel secure and stable. If your dog can't handle free reign of the house (and demonstrates that by destruction or inappropriate elimination), limit him to a room or two and gradually expand his freedom as he becomes more secure.

- *Touch your dog.* Unless your dog is so fearful as to not tolerate your touch, spend quiet quality time with her, gently massaging her or doing Tellington TTouch. Your touch will be calming and will help build your bond.

- *Take him to training classes.* A positive training class will help your dog build confidence, help develop a common language for the two of you, and help build your bond. It will also allow you to spend quality, dog-focused time together. If you're not sure whether your dog is able to handle being around the other dogs in class, talk with your instructor about evaluating him privately in advance.

- *Give her a den of her own.* Many dogs find a crate to be a safe, secure place to hang out. It's also a place to confine your dog temporarily to keep her out of trouble. Be sure to at least give your dog the option of using a crate. (See the chapter on crate training for tips on introducing it.)

- *Try a flower essence.* Flower essences like White Crocus or Gentian from Anaflora or Cosmos from Flower Essence Services can help your new dog get through the emotionally tumultuous first few days or weeks in his new home.

- *Talk to a professional.* If you are having problems with your new adult dog, talk to a trainer or a behaviorist before writing her off. Your dog is surely worth a little extra effort.

- *Love your dog.* Love is the most powerful language of all. Love your dog, without forcing any unwanted attention on him, and he will respond.

HOW NOT TO SAY IT

- *Don't place unrealistic expectations on your dog.* If you've had a dog before, don't expect this new dog to fill the old dog's paw prints exactly. Respect your new dog's individuality. Recognize her current uncertainty about her situation and cut her some slack.

- *Don't punish your new dog.* Now is the time for patience. If your dog does something that's not to your liking, it might be just because he didn't know it would be a problem. If you catch your dog in the act of doing something wrong, be gentle with him. Redirect his attention elsewhere. And never, ever punish him after the fact.

- *Don't spend nonstop time with your dog, then leave her alone for hours on end.* Resist the urge to be your dog's constant companion right after you get her. The contrast between that intensive time together and long periods of social isolation will make your leaving to go to work more difficult for your dog. (See the chapter on separation anxiety.)

- *Don't think the worst.* If your dog is a little hand-shy, it doesn't necessarily mean he's been abused. Don't place your dog in the role of victim. Treat him as a whole, emotionally healthy being until you learn for sure otherwise.
- *Don't force yourself on your dog.* If your new dog is feeling overwhelmed or fearful, she might not appreciate being smothered in love or petted all over her body. You'll have a lifetime together. Don't rush things.

chapter three

Boarding

Barry enjoys traveling, but he hates to leave his dog, Smudge, behind. Sometimes it simply can't be helped, though. Barry finds himself avoiding distant vacations because he can't stand to board Smudge. When he does board her, he spends all his time worrying about her.

Vacations should be fun. When you're traveling for fun and pleasure, you shouldn't have to spend your time worrying about your dog's care. You can help alleviate that worry by carefully selecting a boarding kennel or making alternative arrangements for caring for your pet. With a little planning and footwork, you can make traveling without your dog carefree for both of you!

WHAT YOUR DOG IS TRYING TO TELL YOU

- *"This is fun!"* If your dog is happy to stay at the boarding kennel—he walks in with his head and tail high and doesn't kick up a fuss when you leave—pat yourself on the back. You have a well-adjusted, well-socialized dog on your hands, and you've selected a boarding kennel that doesn't stress him.

- *"Don't leave me here!"* If your dog barks and carries on when you leave, it doesn't necessarily mean the kennel isn't a good one. Most dogs just don't like to be left behind.

- *"Let me stay home."* Sometimes an in-home pet-sitter is the best option.

HOW TO SAY IT

- *Do your research.* Ask your dog-loving friends what facilities they use, and visit the facility in advance of your planned vacation. Listen to your gut: If the kennel doesn't feel right to you, don't use it.

- *Talk happily to your dog when you go to the boarding kennel.* Try not to let your worry make her worried, too.

- *Bring your dog's (washable) bed or toys.* This gives him a little piece of home and keeps him company while you're gone. Don't bring along anything irreplaceable.

- *Bring a little piece of you.* Take along one of your unwashed T-shirts so your smell can keep your dog company. She'll probably find it very comforting.

- *Supply your own food.* If your dog is stressed by your absence, a change in diet might stress his system even more. See if the boarding kennel will let you bring along a supply of his own food.

- *Board them together.* If you have two dogs who get along very well, consider boarding them in the same run so they'll have the pleasure (and comfort) of one another's company.

- *Consider alternatives.* A boarding kennel isn't the only way to have your dog taken care of in your absence. You can hire a pet-sitter to stay in your home, or you can have your dog stay in a pet-sitter's home. Again, do your research and make sure the sitter is licensed and bonded or someone extremely trustworthy. Check references. The National Association of Professional Pet Sitters is a good place to start your search for a pet-sitter. (See the appendix for contact information.)

- *Talk to your vet.* If your dog has a chronic illness, talk to your vet about boarding her at the vet hospital, or perhaps hire a vet tech to come stay at your house to care for your dog.

- *Swap pet care with friends.* If your dog has a good friend, perhaps that dog's family will be willing to care for your dog for you, in exchange for your doing the same for them. Your leaving can actually become a fun time for your dog.

- *Leave written, not just oral, instructions at the boarding kennel or for the pet-sitter.* Try to cover all your bases.

- *Check up on them.* No matter what arrangements you make for your dog, don't be shy about calling the caregiver for updates. There may be small issues that the caregiver wouldn't want to phone you about but that you'd like to weigh in on.

- *Talk to your dog.* Before you leave on your trip, tell your dog what's what. Let him know where you are going and why, who he'll be staying with, and when you'll be back. You'd be surprised at how much dogs understand, and the little time it takes to do this might provide a great comfort to him.

HOW NOT TO SAY IT

- *Don't just have someone look in on your dog.* Dogs are social animals who do not enjoy long stretches of time alone. Don't hire the neighbor kid, or a professional pet-sitter for that matter, to come in and let your dog out or walk her on a daily basis. She needs the company and comfort of a human presence in the house during the hours she's accustomed to it. If you leave her alone 23 hours out of the day, she might compensate by destroying the house.

- *Don't automatically vaccinate.* Many boarding kennels will say they require proof of annual vaccination. But if your dog is older or not completely healthy, it might not be wise to vaccinate him. Ask the kennel if they'll accept titers—a blood test that shows if your dog has enough antibodies in his bloodstream from prior vaccinations to protect him should he be exposed to disease. Because annual vaccinations are becoming increasingly controversial, more boarding kennels will no doubt be accepting titers. (See the chapter on vaccinations for more information.)

- *Don't let price necessarily be your guide.* This isn't a time to cut corners; price shouldn't be the number-one factor in your decision. Rather, cleanliness, access to the outdoors, the kindness of the staff, and the kennel's policies should rank high on your list of considerations.
- *Don't trust your pet to just anyone.* The neighbor kid might seem willing to care for your dog, but will he keep his commitment? Can he be trusted to show up as promised or to not lose your dog? Dog-care professionals (like pet-sitters, vet techs, or trainers who also pet-sit) might detect a problem that your neighbor would overlook.
- *Don't sneak away.* If you try to pack while your dog's not home or surreptitiously leave without telling your dog that you'll be boarding her, you're denying her the opportunity to prepare. Don't take her by surprise; keep her in the loop.

chapter four

Bringing Home Puppy

Margaret and Brian eagerly anticipated the arrival of their Australian Shepherd puppy, Mo. They'd researched the breed, carefully selected the breeder, put a deposit on a puppy before he was even born, and finally they brought the eight-week-old ball of fluff home.

Within a week, they were ready to tear their hair out. Thanks to Mo, they were sleep-deprived, cranky, and resentful that their new little family member was controlling them, not the other way around.

How such a little creature can turn your life—and house—upside down is a mystery. But it doesn't need to be that way. If you prepare for your puppy and follow a few guidelines, your new bundle of joy can be a source of elation rather than frustration. And before you know it, you'll have a wonderful adult companion.

WHAT YOUR DOG IS TRYING TO TELL YOU

- *"I'm just a baby."* A puppy will come into your household knowing little more than a human toddler. Her mom and littermates will, in all likelihood, have taught her some important lessons, but it's up to you to teach her how to be well mannered in the house.

- *"Life is good!"* Puppies revel in being puppies. They know no boundaries, know no rules, and will do anything they please. Your job is to help your puppy channel his exuberance into activities that are pleasing to you.

- *"Why shouldn't I?"* Anything's fair game for a puppy. She'll chew what you leave out. She'll poop and pee wherever she happens to be when the need hits. Puppy mistakes are really your mistakes.

HOW TO SAY IT

- *Prepare for your puppy.* Before you bring your puppy home, do some reading to know what to expect and how to react. (See the appendix for some suggestions on some great general-care and training books). The books of Ian Dunbar, in particular, will help you get a great start with your puppy.

- *Confine your puppy.* An unhousetrained puppy should not be given the run of the house. Set up both a long-term confinement area (like a baby-gated bathroom or kitchen or an escape-proof exercise pen) and a short-term one (a crate). You'll use the long-term confinement area when you're not at home to keep your puppy safe. The crate will help with housetraining. (See the chapters on housetraining and crate training.)

- *Develop a chew-toy habit.* Give your puppy lots of stuffed chew-toys to enjoy. You can even feed her meals in them. If your puppy becomes addicted to chew-toys—and is given an ample supply—she'll be much less likely to chew up your furniture.

- *Socialize your puppy.* Now's the time for your puppy to meet new people and other dogs. Have people over to meet the puppy. Invite dog-loving people of both genders as well as different ages and races. Make sure they interact with the puppy and that only good things come from those people. This early socialization will help your puppy realize his full potential as an adult dog. (See the chapter on socialization for more information on the importance of socializing your puppy.)

- *Talk to your puppy and help her understand your language.* As you become connected, you'll find that she understands more and more of what you say to her.

- *Touch your puppy.* Touching your puppy all over his body will get him acclimated to being touched—your vet and groomer will thank you for it. It will also help you and your puppy bond.
- *Focus on the positive.* Rather than always telling your puppy what not to do, show her what you want her to do. Keep your clicker and treats handy and click her when you see desirable behaviors.
- *Enroll in puppy kindergarten.* Seek out a positive puppy class so your pup can play with other puppies and so your questions can be answered and any problems addressed.
- *Take tons of pictures.* Puppyhood goes by in a flash. Document it while you have the chance, and you'll have years of enjoyment looking at puppy pictures.

HOW NOT TO SAY IT

- *Don't forget that she's a baby.* Puppy mistakes should be highly forgivable. Just show her what you'd rather she be doing. Remember, you're her teacher and her benevolent leader. Don't lose your temper.
- *Don't give him too much freedom.* You need to manage your puppy so he won't become a wee canine tornado wreaking havoc throughout your house. Confine him in a puppy-proof zone, keep him busy, and show him what you want by rewarding him for doing the right thing.
- *Don't abuse the crate.* The crate should be for short-term confinement only. You lose it as a housetraining tool if you leave your puppy in it so long that she's forced to wet or soil the crate. If you must be away from your puppy for hours on end, put her in a long-term confinement area with newspaper, a litter box, or other place she's allowed to go to the bathroom. (See the chapter on housetraining in Part Three.)
- *Don't ignore your puppy.* Pups need lots of playtime and attention. Puppies left to their own devices get into trouble.

chapter five

Dogs and Kids

When Mary and Steve found out they were expecting a baby, they were overjoyed. For five years, their "baby" had been their Yorkie, Simon, and now they were expanding their family further. Being devoted dog owners, the couple was committed to keeping Simon, of course, but they wanted to make the addition of a baby as easy as possible for him.

Kids and dogs are a classic combination. You can make living with kids easier for your dog by preparing him for the impending arrival and setting up some rules that will make everyone's life easier. It's also imperative that you teach kids to respect dogs.

WHAT YOUR DOG IS TRYING TO TELL YOU

- *"What about me?"* For a dog who is used to having his humans' undivided attention, the addition of a baby (or even a visit from a child) can be frustrating. He might do everything in his power to get your attention.
- *"I still have the same needs."* Even if you're busy with a new baby, your dog needs exercise, care, and attention. Try to work out a schedule so your dog isn't neglected.

- *"Everything's changing so fast."* Use the months you have to prepare for a child to help your dog. If you're going to be changing the rules, start early so your dog's accustomed to them by the time the baby arrives.

- *"A playmate!"* Dogs who are unfamiliar with children might get a little rough while playing with them. Always supervise your dog when he's around small children. You don't want your dog to treat a toddler like she's another dog!

HOW TO SAY IT

- *Decide what your limits need to be.* A new baby might mean you need to change the rules for your dog. For example, if your dog is allowed to jump on your lap at any time, you probably won't want her to do that when you have the baby in your lap. So you'll need to teach your dog now that she must sit next to you. When your dog jumps on your lap, say "Oops!" and put her where you want her, then reward her. Remember, you're changing the rules on her, so be gentle and patient.

- *Brush up on your training.* If your dog hasn't been to school yet, take him there before the baby arrives. If he has been to school, brush up on "Sit," "Down," "Stay," and "Leave it." This will be invaluable when you're trying to control his interactions with the baby. If he doesn't know it already, teach him to go to his bed when you ask him to.

- *Crate train.* If your dog isn't used to going into a crate when you're home, start getting her acclimated to it. Put in a stuffed Kong (a virtually indestructible hollow rubber toy that you can stuff with goodies) for her to chew on, and reward quiet behavior. Ignore barking or whining. (See the chapter on crate training for more information.) The crate will provide a safe haven for your dog to get away from kids, and it will allow you to keep your dog out of trouble when you need to focus your attention on the baby.

- *Tell your dog about the new baby.* Let your dog in on the big secret, and he may be taken less by surprise by the arrival of the new bundle.

- *Be calm during introductions.* When your dog meets a new baby for the first time (or a child, for that matter), stay relaxed during the introduction, but be ready to tell your dog to leave it if he tries to get too familiar with the baby. Your dog takes his cue from you, so if you act tense about the first meeting, he might view the baby with some wariness. Be upbeat and praise your dog for his pleasant attention to the baby.

- *Train the kids.* Teach your kids how to behave around dogs. They should know never to run from a dog if they don't want to be chased, nor to poke or prod a dog. They need to respect the crate as the dog's personal space, where she should never be bothered. Teach them to always treat dogs with gentle kindness.

HOW NOT TO SAY IT

- *Don't allow small kids and dogs to be together without supervision.* One mistake on the part of a child—a finger in the dog's eye, for example—and the dog could bite. That can be very dangerous for both child and dog. Don't allow that kind of mistake to happen. Teach your children how to behave around dogs (and vice versa), but don't trust them to behave 100 percent of the time. Supervise them.

- *Don't ignore your dog!* Make sure your dog gets plenty of attention after the baby arrives. Plan ahead to enlist the help of friends to exercise your dog during the first few weeks when you're both busy and sleep-deprived. Think of your dog as you would an older child. His needs shouldn't be supplanted by those of the baby.

- *Don't banish your dog to the yard, the laundry room, or his crate.* Remember, your dog didn't choose for you to have kids. With proper training and supervision, your dog and your kids can learn to get along. The crate should be a temporary holding place only. Work with a trainer, if necessary, to integrate your dog into your new lifestyle.

chapter six

Finding a Lost Dog

One day when Hildy answered the doorbell to take a delivery, her Bull Terrier, Levi, squeezed out in hot pursuit of a cat who happened to be in the yard. By the time Hildy could put down the box and run after her dog, he'd vanished. Hildy knew she needed to act fast, but she had no clue what to do next.

Losing a dog is every dog owner's biggest nightmare, and it can happen to even the most conscientious dog owner. The best way to recover a lost dog is to have considered the possibility ahead of time and to be prepared for it. With preparation and persistence, the nightmare can have a happy ending.

WHAT YOUR DOG IS TRYING TO TELL YOU

- *"Find me!"* Depending on how far a dog has wandered, he might not be able to find his way home. If a Good Samaritan has taken him in, getting home might be completely out of his control.

HOW TO SAY IT

- *Make a very descriptive sign.* Prepare some signs in advance (you can now purchase "Lost Dog" signs at pet-supply stores as well), so all you have to do is add a photograph, photocopy the sign, and put them up all over your neighborhood. Make sure the sign has all the pertinent information to help identify your dog like breed, size, markings, gender, and neutering status if the dog is male. Include a clear picture on the sign, and make sure all the information is easy to read, even by people in passing cars.

- *Keep current pictures of your dog.* As your dog ages, make sure you have a good picture of him that you can put on a sign if need be. If your dog's muzzle has grayed with age, the photo should show it. The photo should also clearly show any identifying characteristics.

- *Always keep an ID tag on your dog's collar.* It's your dog's easiest ticket home. You might want to consider putting the word *Reward* on the tag, assuming you're willing to offer a reward for the return of your dog.

- *Consider some form of permanent identification.* ID tags are great because they're easily seen, but they can also come off. A microchip implanted between your dog's shoulder blades provides a permanent, unalterable form of identification, assuming your dog is taken to a place like a shelter or vet's office that has a microchip scanner. Another form of permanent ID is a tattoo. Whichever form you choose, be sure it is linked to a database with your current information. Keep that database updated when you move.

- *Enlist your friends.* Get friends to help you canvass the neighborhood for your lost dog. Someone should stay home by the phone in case your dog is found or comes home on her own. Your cell phone can become your best friend in times like these.

- *Go to your area shelters and look for your dog.* Fill out a lost-dog form. Then go back every day until your dog is found. Don't rely on phone calls to the shelters.

- *Contact area veterinary hospitals.* If your dog was injured when he was out loose (or even if he wasn't), he might have been taken to a veterinarian. Call the vets in the area and describe your dog, or take your lost-dog sign to all area vet hospitals.

- *Put an ad in the paper.* Most newspapers have a lost and found section in their classifieds.
- *Distribute your sign far and wide.* Put it up at the grocery store, give it to all the delivery people who come to your house, and go door to door in your neighborhood. Everyone should know that your dog is lost.
- *Use the Internet.* Several websites (like www.lostdog.com) exist to help people find their lost pets. You can post a lost-dog notice and look at notices for found dogs. It might be a long shot, but no stone should be left unturned.

HOW NOT TO SAY IT

- *Don't waste any time.* Get out there in your neighborhood and look for your dog before she's able to get very far. Be sure to take a collar and leash with you (in case she's somehow lost her collar) as well as tempting treats (in case she's become so frightened she needs extra incentive to come to you).
- *Don't sit back and wait for the phone to ring.* If your dog is lost, you need to take an active approach to finding him. Don't assume that shelters will call you.
- *Don't wait for your dog to come to you.* She might not be able to if she's been injured or if she can't find her way home. Perhaps someone found her and she's inside a house. Go out and try to find her.
- *Don't pay a reward before actually seeing your dog.* Sadly, con artists have been known to prey on people with lost animals, asking that money be sent before the dog is returned. Don't compound your misery by falling victim to these people.

chapter seven

Going to the Groomer

Whenever Marilee takes her Miniature Poodle, Tessa, to the groomer, she always leaves feeling slightly worried. Tessa doesn't like being left behind and barks in protest. Marilee worries about how the groomer is going to handle her dog. She knows that grooming is necessary for Poodles, but she wishes it weren't so stressful.

Professional grooming is essential for many breeds, particularly those, like Poodles, whose coats grow continuously. But with the right groomer—and with the right groomer-client relationship—going to the groomer needn't be a traumatic event for you and your dog.

WHAT YOUR DOG IS TRYING TO TELL YOU

- *"It's scary here!"* Grooming shops can be loud, with all the hair dryers, running water, and other dogs. They can smell funny. And, surely the smell of canine fear is in the air. Look for a gentle, calm groomer who will do her best to make her grooming shop as relaxing a place as possible.

- *"Grooming hurts!"* If you take your dog in with a matted coat, the process of making her tangle-free and beautiful is going to painful. You can minimize pain by brushing your dog between groomings and trimming her nails, if necessary.

- *"Don't leave me!"* Many dogs don't like being dropped off at places. For most dogs, being separated from their humans is difficult—and it's rare that good things happen when they're left behind.

HOW TO SAY IT

- *Groom between groomings.* Just because you have your dog groomed professionally doesn't mean you're completely off the hook for home grooming. Regular brushing can be an enjoyable experience for you and your dog, and one that will build the bond between you. It also gives you the chance to inspect your dog for any new lumps and bumps, which can help you detect disease early. By brushing your dog regularly and removing any mats before they get big, your dog will be more comfortable and his professional grooming will be much easier.

- *Trim those toenails.* The best way to keep a dog's toenails the proper length is to trim them regularly. Because the quick grows with the nail, you can only take off a little at a time. To avoid your dog getting "quicked" (where the toenail is trimmed too short and bleeds) by the groomer, be sure to trim her nails between groomings. (See the chapter on grooming at home for more information.)

- *Handle your dog.* From the time your dog is young (although it's never too old to start), get her used to having her feet handled, as well as her lips (especially Poodles and other breeds whose faces are shaved or trimmed) and ears. That will make your dog less nervous about the groomer handling her.

- *Listen to your dog.* If, after your dog's visited a grooming shop once, he's very hesitant to go back, he might be telling you that his experience was bad. You'll need to know your dog well enough to know when he's protesting on general principle. But if he reacts much more badly on the second or third trip to a groomer than the first, maybe it's time to seek a new groomer.

Groomers

It's important to select your groomer carefully. This person will be responsible for your dog, handling him, asking him to do things he might not want to do, and using sharp implements around him. Don't just rely on a phone call. Visit the grooming shops you're interested in and interview the groomer. Here are some things to look for and questions to ask:

- Are the dogs groomed within your view?
- Is the shop clean? Ask the groomer about her sanitizing procedures.
- Is the groomer gentle with the dogs in her care?
- Does she listen to you, or does she brush off your concerns?
- Do you get a good feeling from her?
- What emergency procedures does she have in place in the event of illness or injury?

Above all, trust your gut instinct. Even if the groomer gives all the right answers, walk away if you have a bad feeling. Choosing a groomer is no less important than selecting a day-care provider for your child.

- *Inspect your dog when you get home from the groomer for any signs of injury, like razor burns or nicks from scissors.* Take note of what you like and don't like about the haircut so you can suggest changes at the next session.
- *Build a relationship with your groomer.* Be pleasant and chatty. Ask questions of your groomer about his or her procedures. Ask how your dog behaved. The answer can reveal a lot about the groomer's attitude toward your dog.

- *Stay positive.* Don't let your own nervousness about leaving your dog affect how your dog feels. Try not to worry about leaving her at the groomer; keep your voice happy and upbeat.

- *Tell him what's going on.* Give your dog some advance warning that you'll be going to the groomer, and reassure him that you'll be coming back for him.

HOW NOT TO SAY IT

- *Don't go too long between groomings.* If you take your dog to the groomer more frequently, each appointment will be shorter and less stressful. If you wait until your dog is a matted mess, the grooming session will be traumatic for him.

- *Don't be shy.* If you have special instructions for your groomer—particularly if you don't want any procedures done that are usually considered standard procedures (like ear plucking or anal sac emptying)—don't hesitate to speak up. And if you don't like your dog's haircut, tell the groomer exactly what you don't like about it. How he or she reacts to that criticism might affect whether you want to go back.

- *Don't insist on staying with your dog.* If you'd like to stay with your dog during grooming and the groomer is willing, that's great. But don't think that just because a groomer says no that he has something to hide. Many dogs are more difficult to groom when their owners are around, and most groomers prefer that you drop off your dog and come back for her later.

chapter eight

Grooming at Home

The long, silky hair of Tristan, a beautiful Irish Setter, should be a joy to brush. But his owner, Claudia, neglects the task, letting Tristan's hair become ensnared with burrs and tangled with vegetation. When she can't stand it any longer, Claudia brushes him and the uncomfortable dog snarls during the session. He doesn't feel much better about his infrequent baths, which can turn into a battle of wills.

Grooming your dog at home is an important part of being a good dog owner. Not only is it important to your dog's health and comfort, but it can also build the bond between the two of you. Even if you take your dog to a professional groomer, you need to tend to certain tasks between grooming, like brushing, nail trimming, and sometimes even an occasional bath if your dog decides to roll in something.

WHAT YOUR DOG IS TRYING TO TELL YOU

- *"Ouch!"* If you delay brushing so long that your dog is tangled or matted, brushing can actually hurt. No wonder he doesn't like it.
- *"This is tedious."* If your grooming session goes on too long, your dog can get bored and want to walk away. Keep your sessions short and enjoyable.

- *"What's in it for me?"* Some dogs need a little extra motivation to participate in a grooming session. Time to break out the treats!
- *"Ahhhhh."* Brushing should feel good. Properly done, with the right equipment and frequency, your dog will luxuriate in a brushing session.

HOW TO SAY IT

- *Use the right equipment.* There are as many types of brushes as there are types of coats on a dog. Be sure you choose the right brush for your dog. A rubber curry comb, for example, is great for a Labrador Retriever, but will do nothing for a Poodle. Your nail-trimming equipment needs to be appropriate to your dog as well.
- *Be patient.* If your dog doesn't settle down during the grooming session, don't get angry. End the session, then start again later (but not too much later). Short, easy sessions are the name of the game.
- *Start young.* Start grooming your dog as soon as you acquire him. If he's a puppy, all the better, although he's never too old to learn to be groomed. You want to condition him to having his body touched and brushed and get him comfortable with the nail clippers.
- *Listen to your dog.* When your dog says the session's over, end it. Even if your dog ends up looking a little lopsided, or if you haven't finished all his nails, you don't want to push him past his limit. Always end the session on a positive note.
- *Brush frequently.* The more often you brush, the easier it will be on the dog. Take advantage of this quality time together.
- *Start from scratch.* If your dog is very matted, it might be easier for you to have a professional shave her down. Once she's mat-free, start brushing her regularly so the task isn't a chore for either of you.
- *Reward good behavior.* Be sure to reward your dog for letting you groom him. The brushing itself might be a reward, but if there's hesitation, bring

out some treats and click and treat for relaxing. In the tub, reward your dog for not struggling. Be on the lookout for the tiniest improvements to reward.

- *Put down a nonstick mat in the tub or on the grooming table.* That way, your dog won't lose her footing. This should make her feel more comfortable with the grooming.

- *Put your hands all over his body.* Check your dog regularly for lumps, swelling, wounds, or abrasions. Talk to your vet if you find anything suspicious. If you're checking regularly, you're likely to detect signs of disease very early, which is as important for dogs as it is for humans.

- *Talk to your dog.* All the while you're brushing, bathing, or trimming nails, talk to your dog in calm, sweet tones. Tell her what you're doing and why. Use this time to build your connection.

- *Try some flower essences.* If your dog is stressed by grooming, give him some Rescue Remedy to calm him.

- *Learn from an expert.* If you have any questions about the best technique to use to brush your particular type of dog, stop in to a grooming shop for advice.

TIPS FOR NAIL TRIMMING

- *Desensitize your dog to the clippers.* Before you intend to actually clip, start getting your dog—no matter what his age—comfortable with the clippers. Have treats handy and lift up his foot. If he doesn't struggle, click and give him a treat. Pick up his foot and spread his toes. More clicks and treats. Continue, adding small steps like gently pulling on the toenails. Then, introduce the clippers. Let your dog sniff them. Touch the clippers to your dog's foot, clicking for calm behavior. Keep the routine upbeat and brief, until he calmly accepts your actually cutting the nail.

- *Watch for the quick.* If your dog has white nails, you can see the darker quick and be careful not to cut it. But if your dog's nails are dark brown or black, you must cut just a little at a time. After each cut, look for a little white spot that will tell you that the quick is near. If you accidentally cut into the dog's quick, your dog might learn to dread nail clipping.

- *Clip frequently.* The quick in a dog's nail grows with the nail. It also recedes a little every time the nail is clipped, so if you trim off a little frequently, you can achieve short nails painlessly. If you don't trim often, the only way to get short nails is to cut into the quick, which can hurt the dog.
- *Use flour to stop bleeding.* If you do accidentally cut into the quick, dip the bleeding nail into a small dish of flour. It'll stop the bleeding without stinging.

HOW NOT TO SAY IT

- *Don't turn grooming into a battle.* If your dog won't sit still, end the session and start later. Next time, be ready to click and treat for even a hint of toleration and keep rewarding as long as the session lasts. Try grooming when your dog is pooped.
- *Don't hurt your dog.* A brush can cause pain if too much pressure is exerted or if it's not the right brush for the dog's coat. A bath temperature shouldn't be too warm or too cold. And you never want to cut into your dog's toenail's quick. Take it slow and easy, and be sure you're using the right equipment. Keep an eye out for any sign of discomfort or pain.
- *Don't lose your temper.* You might get really frustrated that your dog's not cooperating, but don't shout at your dog about it. Again, the name of the game is making the experience as pleasant as possible.

chapter nine

Leadership Issues

Laura's Giant Schnauzer, Ben, is a lovely dog, but he's also a demanding one. When Laura sits on the couch with him, Ben insists that she pet him continuously. When she stops, he whacks her with his paw. Although they've been through training classes, he only holds a stay about half the time she asks him to. And whenever he feels like it, he jumps up and puts his big paws on her shoulders. They get along fine, but Laura can't shake the feeling that he somehow looks down on her.

Human/dog relationships can suffer from leadership issues. Wolves, the ancestors of our dogs, live in a strict pack hierarchy. It is important—and comforting—for a dog to know his position within his own pack (that is, your family). You should be your dog's benevolent leader, not dictator, and he should learn to defer to your wishes.

Being the leader doesn't mean you have to push your dog around or physically throw him onto his back in the outdated alpha roll. It just means your dog needs to look to you for things he wants and defer to your leadership. Luckily, it's pretty easy to be a benevolent leader by following a few simple principles.

WHAT YOUR DOG IS TRYING TO TELL YOU

- *"I'm confused."* Dogs need to know where they fit in. Dogs who aren't natural leaders can become very confused if no leader is apparent, and their behavior can suffer as a result.
- *"Someone has to be in charge!"* If you don't demonstrate to your dog that you're the leader, he might feel the need to take on the role himself. This can be damaging to your relationship.
- *"I'll really show you who's the boss!"* If your dog is a natural leader (which some people call "dominant") and you're inconsistent in your own leadership, your dog might feel the need to take over the top spot.

HOW TO SAY IT

- *Set limits.* Dogs aren't that much different than kids in terms of needing limits set on their behavior. Like children, dogs will try to test those limits, and it's up to you to reinforce them. Knowing what behavior is allowable within the family gives dogs a sense of security. If your dog crosses the line, make sure he's not rewarded for the behavior. Withdraw your attention, then turn the situation around and ask him to do something for which you can reward him. Giving him a time-out by removing him from the situation and leaving him alone in a room is as much correction as you should need.
- *Teach him that Nothing in Life Is Free.* If you're experiencing leadership issues with your dog, help him recognize that all good things come from you—and they have to be earned. Ask him to sit (or do something else) before you feed him, before you let him out, before you throw his ball, or before he's allowed to do anything else he enjoys.
- *Be consistent.* Setting limits won't do any good if the limits are constantly changing. Set rules and stick to them. If your dog is supposed to lie on his bed while you're eating dinner, he should do that whenever you eat dinner, not just the nights you have guests.
- *Turn a demand around.* If your dog is demanding something from you (for example, she's nudging your hand to try to get you to pet her), don't just do

as she asks. Rather, make your dog's desire a reward. Instead of petting your dog on demand, ask her to lie down, sit, or do a trick, then pet her.

- *Train your dog.* Training is a great way to open the lines of communication between you and your dog and to practice your leadership with your dog. Through positive-reinforcement training, your dog will want to sit, lie down, and stay at your bidding—and come when you call him. What a great way to be a leader.

- *Turn every interaction into an opportunity.* Use your daily interactions with your dog as an opportunity to reinforce your leadership. Feel like giving your dog a treat? Don't just hand over a treat. Ask your dog to sit first.

- *Use your body.* Dogs communicate with one another physically, using their bodies to push one another around. You can do the same (without injuring or frightening your dog) by simply turning your back when your dog jumps on you or by pulling your arms in and turning your shoulder on the dog who jumps on you when you're sitting on the couch. This is more effective than pushing your dog with your hands.

- *Seek professional help.* If your dog is trying to take over as leader and is showing any signs of aggression, don't try to fix the situation on your own. Call in a behaviorist or trainer who specializes in treating aggression to help you establish a program to get your relationship back in line. Make sure the professional uses positive methods. You don't want your dog to hurt you, and you don't want to hurt your dog. Your veterinarian might be able to recommend a behaviorist.

- *Choose sleeping quarters judiciously.* If you have a dog who is always wanting to assert himself as leader, you'd be wise to not allow him to sleep on your bed. By sleeping in the comfy bed yourself and having your dog on the floor, you have exalted status. If your dog tries to insist on sleeping on the bed or climbs up in the middle of the night, have him sleep in a crate at night or tether him to the base of the bed. Note: If you don't have leadership issues with your dog and you want him to sleep on the bed with you, that's perfectly fine.

HOW NOT TO SAY IT

- *Don't give in to your dog's demands.* If your dog is pawing you for attention or whining for a treat, don't reward the behavior by giving him what he wants just to quiet him down. Instead, walk away from your dog, then call him to you and get him to do something for you. Then you can give him a treat or attention.

- *Don't rely on the leash.* Although a leash is an important safety tool when you're outside the house or fenced yard, you should be able to control your dog without it. Establishing and reinforcing your leadership role through training and daily interactions will help you control your dog's behavior when he's off (and on) leash.

- *Don't push or pull at your dog.* Motivate your dog to do what you want through positive training techniques. If your leadership is in question and you try to physically manipulate your dog, you might get bitten. For example, if your dog climbs on the bed and you want him off, don't grab his collar and drag him. That can be a recipe for disaster. Instead, call him to you and give him a treat for coming. Or toss a treat on the floor. Then make a nice bed for him on the floor or in a crate and reward him for using it.

chapter ten

Moving

Andrew and Susan were very excited about Susan's new promotion and their move to a new city. But they worried about how to make the move as stress-free as possible for their sensitive Pomeranian, Stacy. They didn't know how Stacy would handle the packing of the house, the hubbub of moving day, or getting acclimated to their new home.

Moving can indeed be very stressful for dogs (it certainly is for humans!), and it's fraught with potential dangers. With good advance planning, however, and the generous application of common sense, you can make your move easier on your dog—and therefore easier on you.

WHAT YOUR DOG IS TRYING TO TELL YOU

- *"What's going on?"* The activity surrounding moving—packing, throwing things away, accumulating boxes, elevated stress levels—does not escape your dog's notice.
- *"Am I coming with you?"* It's natural for some dogs to worry that they're not going to be included on the adventure. A little reassurance can go a long way in helping alleviate that stress.

- *"Let me help."* Some dogs see you tearing through your belongings and see the piles left out, then decide they can help by going through your stuff themselves.

HOW TO SAY IT

- *Talk to him.* Tell your dog what's going on, so the whole change in routine isn't a big mystery. Even if your dog doesn't understand your words, your intention will likely come through.
- *Keep her safe.* Safety should be a top priority. This means proper identification on your trip (see the chapter on traveling with your dog) is essential. And it means, very importantly, that you eliminate any chance that your dog will escape on moving day.
- *Get him out of the house.* Taking your dog away from the house on move-out and move-in day will ensure that your dog doesn't escape through a door your mover has left open. And it will spare him seeing you stressed out on moving day. It will also reduce your stress—it's one less thing to worry about on an already hectic day. See if your dog can stay with a friend, or take him to doggie daycare, if it's available.
- *Get the movers to pack you.* If it's an affordable option, having the movers pack your belongings will shorten the amount of disruption in your household, making it easier for you and your dog.
- *Give her some flower essences.* Bach's Rescue Remedy will help take the edge off your dog's stress. Don't wait until moving day—add it to her water as soon as you start packing. You might want to take some yourself. In addition, Anaflora makes a flower essence called Relocation that helps animals deal with the stress of a move.
- *Cut him some slack.* If your dog acts out during this stressful time, don't get too upset with him. His life's turning upside down and, unlike you, he has no control over it.
- *Take her to see the new house.* If your move isn't a distant one, take your dog over to inspect the new premises before you move in. That way it won't be so foreign to her on move-in day.

- *Let him get used to being alone in the new house.* If you're taking some time off after the move, don't spend all your time with your dog. When you leave to go to work for a full day, you'll be pulling the rug out from under him. So leave him alone in the new place for an hour or two at a time to get him used to being there by himself. Remember, in the new house, you're the only constant in his life.

HOW NOT TO SAY IT

- *Don't ignore your dog's needs.* There's so much going on during a move that it's easy to forget about one of the less-demanding family members. But dogs need reassurances during stressful times—and they need attention (and exercise) from their humans even during the busiest of times.

- *Don't put your dog in the yard on moving day.* You'll be too busy to supervise her, and there couldn't be a worse day for her to escape. It's much safer to get her off the premises.

- *Don't leave your dog in the house on moving day.* Even if you lock him in a room, you have strangers in the house opening doors. All it would take would be one tragic mistake on the part of a mover and your dog could bolt out the propped-open front door.

- *Don't leave stuff lying around that you don't want your dog to get to.* If your dog is stressed by the packing activities, chewing is a natural anxiety reliever. It's tempting to empty a closet and quit before you've finished packing it. If you do, you might be asking for some dog-related damage.

- *Don't let tempers flare.* It's easy to get irritated with other family members during a move and its preparations. But arguing can really disturb your dog. Start packing early and do it smoothly. Keep things as low-key as possible, for your dog's sake. It'll keep your stress level low, too!

- *Don't put your dog's special things on the moving truck.* Her food and water bowls, favorite toys, and bed should go in the car with you so they can be unpacked right away. This will provide reassuring smells and the comfort of the familiar in a new place.

chapter eleven

Socialization

When you bring your puppy home you're offered a golden window of opportunity during which you can expose your puppy to all manner of life's offerings, which he'll absorb like a sponge. The more you expose your puppy to people of all ages, races, and both genders, the more comfortable he'll be around new people and experiences when he's an adult. If your dog gets to go places, meet other dogs, and see new things while he's a puppy, he'll become a well-adjusted, friendly adult dog who is at ease in all situations. You'll be able to take him anywhere.

Socialization is probably the most important thing you can do for your dog. Without it, he won't be able to reach his full potential. The earlier you start, the better. That first month a new puppy is in his new home (from the age of eight to twelve weeks) is prime time for socialization—don't squander it. But what if it's too late and your dog is already a timid, nervous adult because he wasn't well socialized as a pup? You can still help make the world a more comfortable place for him.

WHAT YOUR DOG IS TRYING TO TELL YOU

- *"Let me see everything."* If your dog isn't a fearful dog (and most puppies aren't), he'll be excited to get out into the world and meet new people or have visitors come to the house.
- *"Help me get over my fears."* If your adult dog is undersocialized and fearful, you can use a system of counterconditioning and desensitization to help her deal with her fears.

HOW TO SAY IT

If Your Dog Is a Puppy

- *Invite people over.* During that first month with your puppy, invite people over in groups for puppy parties. Have the guests hand-feed your puppy his supper, using the food to lure him into sits and downs and feeding the puppy when he comes when called. Ian Dunbar, veterinary behaviorist and author of several books, including *How to Teach a New Dog Old Tricks*, advises that the puppy meet 100 new people during the first month in his new home. That's not as daunting as it sounds: Dunbar describes a systematic socialization program in his books. It's fun for you and fun for the pup, but make no mistake: It's also crucially important. Dunbar believes that not properly socializing a puppy is the biggest mistake a dog owner can make.
- *If you can't have people in, get your puppy out.* If puppy parties are not viable, take your puppy to the park and hold her in your lap. If she doesn't walk around, she's less likely to pick up disease. If you hold your puppy in your lap and put a welcoming expression on your face, people will flock to you. Encourage them to pet your puppy; bring along treats for them to give the pup.
- *Take your puppy to class.* A big concern among veterinarians is that puppies not go out into the world until they're fully vaccinated. But a puppy kindergarten class is a relatively safe environment, since all participants are required to be vaccinated. In these classes, the puppy is exposed to new things, including other dogs and new people, and the teacher will help you address individual questions about your new puppy.

- *Arrange some play dates for your puppy.* Ask people with gentle dogs over to play with your puppy. The dogs can be of different ages and should be of different breeds to maximize your puppy's comfort with all types of dogs. It's an important socialization time, and it's also a great way to tire out your pup.

If Your Dog Is an Undersocialized Adult

- *Click and treat for calm behavior.* When you see your dog being brave, click and treat. Reward even the tiniest sign of courage in the face of something scary.
- *Identify his fears.* Write down the things that scare your dog so you can develop a plan to address those fear triggers.
- *Work on gradually desensitizing your dog to the fear triggers.* Start with the trigger as far away as necessary so your dog doesn't have a fearful reaction and click and treat for calm behavior. See if you can get your dog a little closer to the scary thing. Watch for calming signals that indicate your dog is getting uncomfortable. Very gradually, over the course of multiple training sessions, get closer and closer to the fear trigger until your dog is desensitized to it.
- *Use counterconditioning in conjunction with desensitization.* Change your dog's negative association toward the things she's afraid of. Give your dog a treat in the presence of the fear trigger (for example, tall men or big, black dogs), no matter what your dog is doing. Don't worry if you feel that you're rewarding undesirable behavior. Your goal is for her to eventually see that trigger and look to you for a treat.
- *Talk to a professional if your dog is severely undersocialized.* Some problems are too complex for you to deal with on your own. Severely undersocialized dogs can be a danger to the community. Don't hesitate to seek professional counsel if you're afraid your dog will bite.

HOW NOT TO SAY IT

- *Don't isolate your puppy because you're worried about disease.* Some veterinarians will discourage you from taking your puppy to kindergarten, or even letting him leave your yard, for fear he'll catch a disease. If you listen to that logic, you're risking your dog's future happiness. Not socializing your dog is almost guaranteed to have negative repercussions on his life. You need to weigh the risk of that against the possibility he'll contract a contagious disease. Because the strength of the immunity passed on by the mother is not known, even if he's up-to-date on his vaccinations, there's still a chance he could get a disease out in the world. But if you take him to a relatively safe environment like a puppy kindergarten, you make sure he gets crucial socialization with little risk. You can also socialize your dog safely by having people into your house to meet your puppy.

- *Don't be too overprotective of your puppy.* When your pup is playing with other dogs, try not to get too worried that he's going to get hurt. If your puppy yelps, she's communicating to the other dog that she's frightened or has had enough. Let her do the talking. Give the other dog the opportunity to back off. If he doesn't listen to your puppy, you can gently intervene. Bear in mind that this dog might not be a good future playmate for your pup.

- *Don't isolate your undersocialized adult.* As tempting as it is to protect your dog from the things that scare him by never letting him leave your house, you'll actually be doing him a much bigger favor by getting him out and helping him conquer his fears.

- *Don't coddle your timid dog.* If you coo and reassure your dog whenever she shows fear, you're actually rewarding the fear. (See the chapter on shyness for more information.)

chapter twelve

Traveling with Your Dog

Jerry hates to go on vacation without his Pointer, Spot, but he doesn't know whether Spot would make a good traveling companion or if he'd even be able to find a hotel that would accept dogs. And he is afraid that something bad might happen to his dog while they're away.

Many dogs travel very well. Once you get plugged into the world of dog-friendly travel, it's not hard to find destinations where you can bring your dog along. Remember that when traveling with your dog, safety is paramount. Losing a dog while traveling is unthinkable.

WHAT YOUR DOG IS TRYING TO TELL YOU

- *"May I come?"* Most dogs would love to take a trip with their human. If your dog is at ease with new people and new surroundings and travels calmly in the car, he's a good candidate for the family vacation.

- *"I'm better off at home."* Some dogs just aren't good travelers. These include dogs who are aggressive with strangers, who become anxious in unfamiliar surroundings, and who are extremely stressed in the car.

HOW TO SAY IT

- *Properly identify him.* If your dog were to get lost while you were traveling, his regular collar tag with his home address and phone number wouldn't help much. Create a special travel tag with your cell phone number and an emergency number, or use a paper key tag and a permanent marker to make a temporary tag with the phone number where you're staying. You can make a new one for each night on the road if you're on the move. Or try the Jiffy Tag, a waterproof tag you can write on with a pen, available for only 50 cents each from Animal Care Equipment and Services, Inc. (See the appendix for contact information.)

- *Bring her own food and water.* Diarrhea can make traveling difficult for both you and your dog. Bring along a supply of your dog's regular food to minimize stomach upset. If your dog is particularly sensitive, bring along some bottled water or tap water from home, because tap water can vary from place to place.

- *Restrain him in the car.* There are many types of car restraints now available for dogs, from harnesses that attach to the car's seatbelt, to dog car seats, crates, and barriers. It's as important for your dog to be protected in case of collision as it is for your human passengers.

- *Don't put your dogs near air bags.* If your car is equipped with front-seat air bags, be sure your dog is in the backseat. Air bags can smother dogs, just like they can small children.

- *Be a good citizen.* Always pick up after your dog when you're walking her, whether you're at home or away. If you allow your dog on the bed in a hotel room, bring along a sheet from home for her to lie on so you don't leave behind dog hair. If your dog barks when left alone in a hotel room, don't leave her alone. Order room service and eat in with your dog, or go through a drive-thru.

- *Choose your destinations carefully.* Some vacations can be completely dog-oriented, like the growing number of vacation camps for dogs and their

Dog Talk

Air Travel

Air travel—is it safe? That depends on whom you ask. If your dog is small enough to fit in a carrier under the seat in front of you, then it's probably fine, assuming your dog has the temperament for flying and won't be disruptive. If your dog is large and must be flown in cargo, caution is advisable. The safety of air travel depends on many factors, including the temperature, layovers, and your dog's health and temperament. If you decide to fly with your dog in the cargo hold, be sure to make advance arrangements with the airline, know all their rules so you don't encounter a difficult situation upon check-in, and try to get a nonstop flight. Give air travel a great deal of thought before proceeding. Tragedies have been known to happen. For example, in 2001, one of the top Samoyed show dogs in the country froze to death in the cargo hold of an airplane. If that can happen to a highly trained and valuable dog, it can happen to your dog.

owners. Others can pleasantly accommodate a dog. But if you're taking a family vacation that involves multiple visits to places like amusement parks that don't allow dogs, do your dog a favor and leave him at home.

- *Bring along a little piece of home.* Bring your dog's crate (if she likes a crate and it's easily transportable) or her bed so she'll have a familiar place to rest in unfamiliar surroundings. Doggone Good makes a nylon mesh Cabana crate that's lightweight and easy to put up and break down. (See the appendix for contact information.)

HOW NOT TO SAY IT

- *Don't leave your dog in the car for long.* In warm weather, the car can heat up to deadly temperatures within minutes. If you have to stop at a rest area on a warm day, blast the car's air conditioning as you approach the rest stop. Then dash in and use the facilities before letting your dog out to relieve himself. Always park in the shade and minimize the time your dog is left alone in the car.

- *Don't sedate your dog.* If you're flying your dog, it might be tempting to sedate her. However, sedation can affect your dog's breathing, which can become an issue at high altitudes. Instead, try flower essences, like Rescue Remedy, which can safely calm your dog.
- *Don't let your dog run loose.* Even if your dog is reliable off-leash, unless you're in a securely fenced area, don't risk losing him in an unfamiliar place by letting him run loose.
- *Don't assume everybody likes your dog.* You might have the friendliest dog in the world, but some people just dislike dogs. Don't force your dog on others while you're traveling.

part two

Keeping Your Dog Healthy and Safe

Just as there's been a revolution in dog training from punishment-based methods toward positive-reinforcement-based methods, there's been a shift in thinking by many progressive dog owners about their dog's health care. People have begun questioning the need for routine annual re-vaccination, for example. More dog owners are preparing their dogs' food at home, or are at least scrutinizing the labels of the commercial dog food for better ingredients. Holistic veterinarians are becoming increasingly popular as people seek ways to keep their dogs healthy or look for alternative ways to treat serious illness.

The best way you can help your dog's health is to listen to him. If he tells you he isn't feeling well, pay attention, even if the clues are very subtle. Build a relationship with your veterinarian so you're not embarrassed to call and say that something's just not right. Look for a vet who listens to every comment you make about changes in your dog. You know your dog better than anyone, and your observations are the basis upon which your veterinarian makes treatment recommendations.

Taking good care of your dog's health is much like taking care of your own. If your dog becomes ill, research the illness so you can ask educated questions of your veterinarian. Get a second opinion, if you think it's warranted. Apply critical thinking when your vet makes recommendations, rather than accepting them automatically. You are your dog's advocate.

Along with keeping your dog healthy, you want to keep him safe. A little paranoia can be a good thing, because freak accidents do occur. Think about worst-case scenarios and do what you can to minimize any possible dangers. Your dog is depending on you.

chapter thirteen

Diet

Bob's Brittany, Taffy, itches all the time. She scratches herself and chews on her paws and often seems just miserable. Bob feels bad for Taffy—and loses sleep because Taffy's scratching in the night wakes him up. Although he's bathed her in special oatmeal baths and given her Benadryl, he hasn't yet tried one thing that might really help Taffy: a change in diet.

That old axiom "You are what you eat" applies to dogs as much as it applies to humans. Good nutrition is the cornerstone of good health. When dogs suffer from poor nutrition (or from food allergies) it often shows up in a dull, flaky coat; itchiness; gastrointestinal upset; and general ill health. And sometimes, poor nutrition is the culprit when a dog has behavior problems.

Commercial dog foods purport to be "complete and balanced," yet there is a huge disparity between different foods. Being aware of dog food ingredients, buying the best dog food you can afford, or even preparing your dog's food yourself can help keep your dog in tip-top shape.

WHAT YOUR DOG IS TRYING TO TELL YOU

- *"This food isn't giving me what I need."* If your dog isn't vibrant or suffers from low-grade chronic illness, perhaps you need to switch to a higher-quality food.
- *"My food makes me feel bad."* If your dog is sensitive or allergic to a component of his food, be it a food ingredient or an additive, his food can actually make him sick.
- *"How about some variety?"* For years, veterinarians and pet food manufacturers insisted that dogs don't need variety in their diet and that it was best to stick to one brand of food. It would be like your eating nothing but one brand of cereal every single day. Holistic vets advocate lots of variety in a dog's diet. Dogs crave variety—and their bodies need it.
- *"May I have some of what you're eating?"* If you eat healthfully, don't be afraid to share some of your food with your dog. He'll thank you for it!

HOW TO SAY IT

- *Buy the best you can afford.* Higher-quality ingredients cost more, but high prices don't necessarily equate with high quality. A lot of money can go into marketing and packaging instead of into ingredients.
- *Learn to read a label.* If you're serving your dog commercial dog food, know what's in it. Look for meat (like beef, poultry, or lamb) in the first three ingredients. Avoid food with by-products, particularly the generic "meat by-products." Minimize grains—they're an inexpensive source of protein, but dogs aren't built to process them well. Avoid any food with sugar and flavoring added and with artificial preservatives. (See the appendix for further reading on pet food ingredients.)
- *Do your research.* If you decide that you'd like to prepare your dog's food yourself, don't just jump into it without informing yourself on dog nutrition. For example, a meat-only diet is not healthy for dogs, because it lacks certain minerals like calcium. Dogs need vegetables, but the vegetables must be processed (put through a food processor or cooked) for your dog to

digest them. Learn the basics of canine nutrition so you're providing nutrition that is balanced over time.

- *Supplement with "people food."* If you eat healthfully, your dog will benefit from your sharing a bit of your supper with him. Just make a little extra for the dog. Real, whole food is good for your dog.
- *Try some bones.* Raw bones can be very nutritious for your dog. Crunching on a poultry bone like a chicken back or turkey neck is both enjoyable and nutritious for your dog. Raw bones, like beef knuckle bones, are great natural teeth cleaners, too.
- *Give her a digestive enzyme.* A digestive enzyme like Prozyme, which is made for dogs and cats, or one made for humans and available at a health-food store, will help your dog digest her food better.
- *Look into raw food.* Proponents of raw feeding for dogs point out that cooking depletes food of its vitamins and enzymes. Raw-food diets are closest to a dog's natural diet. If you're interested in trying it, do some research before preparing raw food for your dog. Or buy some prepared raw frozen foods from reputable companies. (See the appendix for companies that sell prepared raw diets.)
- *Talk to your veterinarian about food allergies.* If you have an itchy dog, talk with your vet about switching to a food with a protein source your dog hasn't been exposed to before, like rabbit or duck, to see if that helps stop the scratching. Your vet might advise an elimination diet (where you eliminate all but one or two ingredients, then gradually add back more ingredients) to try to determine exactly what your dog is allergic or sensitive to. Some veterinarians will use a blood test to determine food allergies.

HOW NOT TO SAY IT

- *Don't buy the cheapest food for your dog.* Inexpensive food is made from inexpensive ingredients. In general, inexpensive ingredients, like peanut hulls and brewer's rice (the waste product of commercial beer brewing), don't provide good nutrition for your dog.

- *Don't feed cooked bones.* Although raw bones can be beneficial for your dog, cooked bones can splinter and cause choking or tear up your dog's insides.
- *Don't feed "table scraps."* Don't give your dog your dregs, like the gristle from your steak you didn't want. Share the good stuff—the food you actually eat.
- *Don't feed a homemade diet without doing research first.* If you decide to take your dog's nutrition into your own hands, make sure you know what you're doing. Read books, talk to a veterinarian open to home-prepared diets, and talk to others who are doing it. Internet mailing lists are a great way to interact with experienced home feeders. Your dog depends on you to provide him with good nutrition, so make the effort to know what you're doing first. (See the appendix for books on home-prepared diets.)

chapter fourteen

Emergencies

When Pat's Great Dane, Ranger, started pacing around the house, asking urgently to go out, Pat's radar went up. Ranger would lie down, then get right back up again. He tried to vomit, but nothing came out. Pat knew something was wrong, and her instincts told her it might be serious. When she noticed that his belly was slightly distended and felt that it was tight as a drum, she grabbed her cell phone and her car keys. Ranger might be bloating!

Recognizing the symptoms of a medical emergency can make the difference between life and death for your dog. In the case of bloat, where a dog's belly fills with air or gas, sometimes causing his stomach to twist and cut off the blood supply, immediate veterinary care is essential. By being prepared for a medical emergency, knowing your dog well enough to recognize when he's in distress, and trusting your instincts, you might one day save your dog's life.

WHAT YOUR DOG IS TRYING TO TELL YOU

- *"I'm in pain."* The way individual dogs display pain or distress can vary. Try to get to know how your dog acts when he's in pain.

- *"I don't feel well."* Unusual behavior on the part of your dog can be a sign that she's ill.

HOW TO SAY IT

- *Pay attention to your dog.* If you notice that your dog just isn't feeling right, take notes. You know him better than anyone, and the information you provide the veterinarian can be vital.

- *Trust your instincts.* If you think something is wrong with your dog, don't hesitate to call the emergency number for your veterinarian or the emergency clinic. They might give you instructions on home care, but they might also want to see your dog immediately.

- *Stay calm.* If you're faced with a medical emergency with your dog, you can help your dog stay calm by staying calm yourself.

- *Administer some Rescue Remedy.* This Bach flower essence is perfect for calming during traumas. Give a few drops to your dog in her mouth, in her water, rubbed into her ears, or even mixed with water and misted over her. Then take some yourself to help you keep your wits about you.

- *Be prepared.* Know your vet's office hours and emergency-contact procedures. Know where the nearest emergency veterinary hospital is and how long it takes to get there. Post the phone numbers prominently, program them into your cell phone memory, and take your cell phone with you when you walk your dog. It could be a lifesaver.

- *Know your breed's potential problems.* If your dog's breed is prone to particular veterinary emergencies (like bloat, which affects deep-chested dogs), be fully aware of the symptoms so you can act swiftly.

- *Know the signs of shock.* Your dog might be going into shock if his mucous membranes (like his gums) become very pale, if the refill time when you press on the gums is slow (more than two seconds to go back to pink from white), if he's dehydrated (his gums feel tacky), or if he's weak or disoriented. If your dog goes into shock, take him to the veterinarian immedi-

Dog Talk

First-Aid Kits

Keep a first-aid kit for your pet in your house and in your car. You can buy one ready-made, or you can make one from items you can purchase at the drug store. At a minimum, your first-aid kit should contain the following:

- Gauze sponges
- Gauze bandage
- Gauze pads
- Vet wrap (stretchy, adhesive gauze that adheres to itself)
- Adhesive tape
- Scissors
- Tweezers
- Antiseptic solution like Betadine
- Hydrogen peroxide (to induce vomiting)
- Thermometer
- Latex gloves
- Ice pack (the type you can break for instant cold)
- Saline solution for cleaning wounds
- Appropriate-size cloth muzzle

Talk with your veterinarian about other items you might need in your first-aid kits.

ately. Ear TTouches can help your dog when he's going into shock. Perform them on the way to the hospital.

- *Pack a first-aid kit.* Keep a first-aid kit in your house and in your car (see the sidebar for recommended contents). Read a book about or take a course in animal first aid, so you know how and when to use the contents of the kit.

HOW NOT TO SAY IT

- *Don't second-guess yourself.* When in doubt, call the vet or go to the hospital. The consequences of not doing so when you have an emergency on your hands are much more severe than the embarrassment you might feel over an unnecessary call.
- *Don't trust your dog not to bite during an emergency.* If your dog is in pain, he might bite you, even if he's never displayed any aggression. Play it safe and put a muzzle on your dog if he's injured.
- *Don't rely on the Internet.* Sending an email to a newsgroup or mailing list is not an effective way to deal with an emergency. Call a professional who can help you immediately.

chapter fifteen

Euthanasia

Brenda knew her Dachshund was dying. Stricken with cancer, Hugo had stopped eating and was extremely lethargic. The thought of having him put to sleep was more than Brenda could bear.

Contemplating the death of your dog is painful at best. But thinking about it in advance can help you make decisions before you're faced with a crisis. Euthanasia can be the last gift you give your dog. Ideally, the procedure is planned and peaceful. Understanding what your options are for euthanasia, and being in tune with your pet so you know when the decision is right, can help you make this time less painful.

WHAT YOUR DOG IS TRYING TO TELL YOU

- *"Life's no longer great."* If your dog's illness results in pain, inability to walk easily, or loss of bowel and urinary control, these might be signs that quality of life has deteriorated to the point where euthanasia is the humane solution.

- *"Please let me go."* If your dog is terminally ill and his quality of life has deteriorated, he'll try to tell you that it's his time to go. Stay connected with him and look for clues in his eyes.

- *"I'd like to die at home."* If your dog gets anxious at the veterinarian's office, or in the car, talk with your vet about the possibility of coming to your house to administer euthanasia. If that's not possible, look for a house-call vet in your community who might be able to help.

HOW TO SAY IT

- *Talk to your dog.* If he's very ill or seriously injured, look into your dog's eyes and ask him to tell you if he's ready to go and if he needs help. Tell him that if he feels it's time to go on his own, that's okay, too. Sometimes dogs will hang on for our sake.

- *Listen to your dog.* Look for indications on her part that death would be a mercy. Although each individual is different, pain, unwillingness to eat, and undignified living conditions might be signs that euthanasia would be welcome.

- *Ask your vet for sedation for your dog.* The lethal solution your vet can give your dog to cause death (an overdose of anesthesia) must be administered intravenously. Because it can be difficult for your vet to find a vein—and the search can be extremely stressful for both you and your dog—ask the vet to sedate your dog with a shot under his skin first. That way, your dog will go into a deep sleep, free of pain, during which you can say your last good-byes. He won't be bothered as your vet looks for a vein.

- *Be prepared for some natural reactions.* Your dog might gasp before dying—a purely physical reaction that doesn't indicate pain or distress. She will also probably empty her bowels and bladder. Again, this is perfectly natural and nothing to feel stressed about.

- *Discuss euthanasia options with your vet in advance.* Find out if she's willing to do the procedure at your home, how much advance notice she needs, and whether there's a particular time of day that works best for her, whether you have the procedure done in the office or at home.

- *Know what you'll do with the remains.* You may wish to bury your dog's body, or you may want to have her cremated. Ask at the vet's office whether they offer private cremation and whether you can get the ashes back. Decide in advance what you'll do with your dog's remains so you don't have to make that important decision under stress.

- *Give yourself permission to grieve.* Losing a dog is like losing a family member. Even if society doesn't understand the depth of your feelings for your dog, you should take the time to grieve and to remember the good life you had together with your dog. See if you can take some time off from work to grieve privately.

- *Seek help in dealing with your loss.* Pet-loss support groups are on the rise. Call your veterinarian or local humane society to see if you can get help from a local organization.

HOW NOT TO SAY IT

- *Don't hold on to your dog just because you can't bear to live without him.* If you know in your heart that he needs help dying, let him go, for his sake, if not yours.

- *Don't assume that a natural death is necessarily better.* It might be preferable for your dog to go on her own, but if she is suffering, exercise the humane alternative that people have for their pets. It can be the last favor you do for your dog.

- *Don't be pressured into euthanasia.* If there's a disagreement among family members about whether it's time to euthanize your dog, try to reach a mutual decision so that resentment doesn't linger. Look to your dog for clues.

chapter sixteen

Excess Weight

Glenn knew that her Basset Hound, Elmo, was putting on a little weight. But when she took Elmo in for his annual check-up, she was shocked to learn that he'd added ten pounds over the past year!

Pounds have a way of sneaking up on us. When you're with your dog every day, it's sometimes hard to notice a thickening of the waist. And it's very difficult to deny a beloved dog some tasty morsels.

Yet being overweight is no more healthy for your dog than it is for you. Because you control what your dog eats, it's up to you to take care of his weight problem. Sometimes just a few dietary substitutions and increased exercise will do the trick.

WHAT YOUR DOG IS TRYING TO TELL YOU

- *"I like to eat!"* Most dogs just love to eat. They don't have a lot of other things going on in their lives, and mealtime is a highlight of the day.
- *"I know a sucker when I see one!"* Dogs are consummate beggars. There's something about those big brown (or blue) eyes that humans can't resist. Those between-meal snacks can really put on the weight.

- *"I'm not well."* Weight gain can be a sign of a number of health problems, most commonly a low thyroid level.

HOW TO SAY IT

- *Exercise your dog more.* As with humans, the key to canine weight loss is to increase exercise and decrease calories. If your dog is seriously overweight, check with your vet about an exercise program so she doesn't overdo it. Show your dog you love her by taking her on more walks, rather than by giving her more food or treats.

- *Change what you feed.* If you feed kibble, switch to a lower-calorie variety (consult with your vet first). If you feed a home-prepared diet, increase the proportion of vegetables (and grains, if you feed them) to meat, making sure you're still feeding a balanced diet.

- *Cut back on the food.* Feed your dog less per meal. If that doesn't seem to satisfy him, add some low-cal, low-fat filler, like green beans or canned pumpkin (not pumpkin pie mix), so your dog won't feel so hungry.

- *Feed her more often.* Eating more smaller meals per day, even if it's less food, will help your dog feel less hungry.

- *Measure your dog's food.* If you're trying to limit the amount you feed, don't eyeball it. Use a measuring cup.

- *Turn supper into a treat.* Reserve some of your dog's regular food to give as treats throughout the day.

- *Treat differently.* Try some lower-calorie treats, like raw or steamed vegetables (if your dog considers them a treat), pieces of rice cake, or low-cal biscuits. Break the treats into tiny pieces. After all, it's not the size of the treat but the fact you're giving the treat that pleases both you and your dog.

- *Have blood tests done.* If your dog's putting on weight, ask your vet to do complete blood and thyroid panels. If your dog's thyroid levels are low, your vet will probably put her on synthetic thyroid hormone, which will make her feel better and help her lose weight.

- *Enlist the whole family.* Your efforts to feed your dog less won't do much good if your kids are slipping her food from the dinner table. All family members must understand the importance of your dog's diet.

HOW NOT TO SAY IT

- *Don't do anything drastic without first consulting your vet.* This includes greatly reducing calories and increasing exercise. You're trying to make your dog healthier, not sicker.

- *Don't underestimate the dangers of being overweight.* Excess weight is particularly hard on arthritic dogs and dogs with any other health problems. It can actually cause health problems, like diabetes.

- *Don't free-feed.* If your dog is accustomed to eating whenever he wants—particularly if you have more than one pet—don't just leave the food out all day. Feed at designated times and remove any opportunity for your dog to steal the other animal's food by supervising all feedings.

- *Don't give in.* Even if your dog is clearly telling you he's absolutely starving (assuming he's eating the appropriate amount of food), don't give in and give him a spoonful of your supper. Instead, give him a tiny bit of rice cake or low-cal dog biscuit. Those little indiscretions can add up. If you really feel that your dog isn't getting enough food to satisfy him, talk with your vet about how much you should be feeding him.

chapter seventeen

Fleas and Ticks

When Nina's Flat-Coated Retriever, Victor, started scratching at himself, she didn't pay that much attention. Then Nina started itching herself. She suspected the worst: fleas. Because Vic was black, it was hard to spot any fleas on him, so she turned him over and looked at the barest part of his body, his belly. There she saw the little critters walking around. After she finished recoiling, she got on the phone with her vet and asked about the best way to rid her dog—and her house—of the nasty little bugs.

Fleas are an enormous nuisance. They're uncomfortable for the dog—and downright dangerous if the dog is allergic to fleabites—and they're difficult to get rid of. Fleas can bring tapeworms and, in severe cases, anemia. Ticks are awful, too, because they spread disease. These days there are newer, easier options for flea and tick prevention. Some more natural nontoxic options can do the trick as well. Don't let fleas and ticks upset you and your dog!

WHAT YOUR DOG IS TRYING TO TELL YOU

- *"Scratch, scratch, scratch . . . this itches!"* Fleas can turn your dog into a scratching fool.

- *"I'm allergic!"* Some dogs suffer from fleabite dermatitis, where they actually have an allergic reaction to the flea's saliva. Those dogs become absolutely miserable after a flea bite, so prevention is essential.

- *"I don't feel well."* If you use a chemical flea preventative, your dog might have a reaction, such as itching, nausea, or abdominal pain. You can avoid these effects as well as any potential long-term effects by using natural flea treatments.

HOW TO SAY IT

- *Inspect your dog for fleas.* If you choose to avoid the flea-prevention chemicals, check your dog once a week during warm-weather flea season by using a flea comb. Comb your dog over something white and look for black specks to come out; they might be flea feces. If you wet and smear the speck and get a reddish smear (from ingested blood), you'll know that it's flea dirt, not just dirt. If you find fleas, act quickly to remove them from your dog and house to prevent an infestation.

- *Inspect your dog for ticks, too.* Ticks can transmit diseases like Lyme disease, Rocky Mountain spotted fever, erlichiosis, and more. It's essential that you remove any ticks you find on your dog. Gently massage your dog regularly—or daily if you walk every day in areas where ticks live—and feel for small bumps. Then part the fur to inspect the bump. If it's attached at one small point (the tick's head), it's probably a tick.

- *Remove ticks pronto!* The sooner you remove the tick, the less chance the tick has to make your dog ill. Ticks must feed for twenty-four to thirty-six hours before they transmit disease. To remove a tick, use tweezers and grasp the tick as close to the dog's skin as possible. Pull out in a smooth, slow motion. Do not twist. Put the tick in some alcohol to kill it. Don't flush it down the toilet, since that might not kill the tick. If you're concerned about disease, save the dead tick to show to your vet. Don't pull the tick out with your bare fingers—if you squeeze the tick too hard, it could transmit disease to you.

- *Make a note.* Mark on your calendar the date you found a tick, its appearance (was it gray and puffed up, bloated with blood?), and how many you found on your dog. The information might be helpful to your vet down the road if your dog gets sick.

- *An ounce of prevention.* Talk with your vet about chemical flea and tick preventatives. There are liquids you can put between your dog's shoulder blades, as well as monthly pills that help control ticks and fleas. If your dog is healthy and on a good diet, he might not need the preventatives—fleas and ticks might not mess with him. If you live in a heavy flea area, you might want to use these chemicals—but be aware that they are pesticides that sometimes make dogs sick and might not be safe for your dog. Frontline works for three months on fleas but only one month on ticks. So if fleas are your problem and you're not taking your dog into the woods or other tick-prone areas, you might be able to get by with only a dose or two in the summer.

- *Remove dormant fleas and eggs by vacuuming frequently.* Concentrate on the areas near your dog's bedding and in high-traffic areas (where the fleas or eggs might be tracked in).

- *Try a natural approach.* Flea treatments do not have to be toxic. A program of thorough cleaning plus the application of some nontoxic supplements can be effective—and safer for you and your dog. It's more labor-intensive than a monthly application of liquid, but if you're interested in minimizing pesticides, it can be worth it. See the excellent article by Kathleen Dudley in the March 2002 issue of *The Whole Dog Journal* for a thorough look at natural integrated pest management. (Ordering information is in the appendix.)

- *Talk to a holistic veterinarian about natural strategies for flea control.* These would include improved diet, supplements like garlic and vitamin B, and natural preparations like certain essential oils or lemon oil you can put on your dog.

- *Treat the environment.* If your dog does end up with a flea problem, you'll have to treat your house and yard as well as your dog. Before bombing the house with chemicals, look into natural approaches to pest control. At the very least, call pest-control companies to find one that will treat with minimally toxic ingredients, like boric acid or sodium polyborate.

HOW NOT TO SAY IT

- *When you remove the tick, don't use a twisting motion.* This might detach the tick's body from its head, leaving the head imbedded in your dog.
- *Don't use Vaseline or matches on ticks.* Don't try to smother or burn the tick. You might just burn your dog! Instead, remove the tick and kill it in alcohol.
- *Don't use preventatives year-round.* There's no need to give your dog flea and tick preventatives if the fleas and ticks are dormant. And unless you live in a very warm climate, they're dormant at least part of the year. You don't want to load his body with unnecessary chemicals.
- *Don't buy over-the-counter flea medicine.* If you decide to give your dog flea chemicals, talk with your vet. The prescription flea preventatives are newer and tend to be safer.
- *Avoid the Lyme vaccine.* The efficacy and safety of this relatively new vaccine is a matter of controversy among veterinarians. Although Lyme disease is a very serious disease in humans, it is less serious for dogs and can be treated with antibiotics.

chapter eighteen

Giving Medication

When Bill's Dalmatian, Sally, was diagnosed with a chronic condition, Bill learned that he'd have to give her a pill twice a day for the rest of her life. He didn't relish the idea of forcing a pill down her mouth each day, but Sally wasn't about to just take the pill out of his hand.

Giving a dog medication needn't be a struggle. Most dogs will gladly take a pill—if you make it tempting enough. Some liquid medications can be put into food. If you can make giving pills a reward itself, you can turn a potentially stressful routine into an easy one.

WHAT YOUR DOG IS TRYING TO TELL YOU

- *"Yum!"* Many dogs eagerly anticipate their daily pill if the pills are hidden in something delectable.
- *"If you say so."* Your dog might allow you to jam the pill down her throat with no fuss. But why put her through that when you can turn a pill into a treat?

- *"Ptooey!"* Some medicines taste so yucky that their bad taste can overshadow even the tastiest wrapping. Talk to your veterinarian about getting the medication in a more palatable form.

HOW TO SAY IT

- *Try tossing the pill into his food.* Some dogs are such chow hounds they'll scarf up pills with their supper. It's worth a try. But be on the lookout for pills that have been spit out.

- *Make it tasty.* There are lots of tasty, sticky substances you can coat a pill with. Things like soft cream cheese (whipped is especially easy), baby food, peanut butter, softened butter, and puréed, cooked liver are all tempting to most dogs. Just drop the pill into the substance, coat it well, and offer it on your finger. Most dogs will happily lick it off. If your dog's on a long course of medication, clear the pill-hiding substance with your vet.

- *Grind the pill.* Buy an inexpensive pill grinder to turn tablets into powder. Assuming that the powder doesn't taste too bad, you can mix this with a small amount of food and it won't leave any suspicious lumps in the food. Similarly, you can empty capsules into food.

- *Try some liquid.* Some medications come in liquid form. Ask your vet if you can put it in food. If not, a simple squirt in the mouth might not be traumatic for your dog if the liquid doesn't taste too bad. Put the liquid in the side of the dog's mouth, rather than squirting it into the back of his throat. You don't want it to go down his windpipe.

- *Get better-tasting medication.* Ask your vet if he or she would be willing to work with a compounding pharmacist to come up with a medication specifically designed to be palatable to your dog. Compounding pharmacists are old-fashioned pharmacists who create custom medications. Many will make liver-flavor chewable pills, for example, or liquid medications in a fish-flavor suspension. If you can turn medicine into a treat, you and your dog will both benefit!

- *Open mouth, insert pill.* If a dog is very ill, his appetite might be flagging and even the tastiest wrapping might be unappealing. In that case, try prying his jaw open and putting the pill right at the back of his tongue. Close his mouth and stroke his throat until you know he's swallowed. This method is more stressful for dogs than those described above, but sometimes it's the best you can do if his taste buds have been turned off.

- *Talk to her.* No matter what method you use, tell your dog what's going on, using soothing tones. Don't grab her and take her by surprise. Your loving intention will come through in your tone and perhaps even your words. You want her to understand that you're doing it for her own good.

- *Reward him.* Unless the pill becomes a treat itself, reward your dog with a treat or special attention once the medication has gone down. Giving him a food treat has the added benefit of making him swallow more, minimizing the chance that you'll find a spit-out pill on the floor hours later.

HOW NOT TO SAY IT

- *Don't make force your first option.* By all means, try to make giving medication to your dog a pleasant experience by hiding it in food or making it a special treat. Resort to manual pilling only if you really have to.

- *Don't fumble.* If you do have to give the pill manually, try to make it as clean and calm a procedure as you can. No big deal—open the mouth, pop in the pill, watch for the swallow. If you turn it into a drama, your dog might never get used to it.

- *Don't chase your dog around in order to grab and pill her.* Make the procedure as low-stress as possible by gently handling your dog and soothingly talking with her about what's about to happen.

- *If your dog hates taking medications, don't call him to you and then give him the medicine.* You really undermine the power of "Come" when you do this. Instead, take the pill to your dog.

- *Don't lose your temper.* It can be very frustrating when your dog struggles while you're trying to do something for her own good. But remember, she's simply being a dog. Losing your temper will only make it more stressful for both of you.

chapter nineteen

Going to the Vet

Mark and Linda's dog, Jackson, hates going to the veterinarian's office. He puts up such a fight that he has to be muzzled so the vet can examine him without fear of being bitten. The whole experience is so hard on Jackson that Mark and Linda hesitate to take him in for wellness exams.

Avoiding the vet's office because your dog hates it can be detrimental to his health. By carefully selecting the vet, helping take some of the fear out of the visit, and taking some precautions so no one is hurt, you can stop avoiding the vet visits and keep your pet healthy.

WHAT YOUR DOG IS TRYING TO TELL YOU

- *"They're going to kill me!"* Some dogs simply distrust the vet. Their first exposure to a vet was probably negative (the puppy got a shot or two), and all sorts of fears and superstitions spring up on every trip back.
- *"I hurt!"* If your dog is injured or ill, he's not going to be his usual, pleasant self. Unfortunately, vets often see dogs at their worst. By helping your dog

trust your vet, you can make those visits when he's feeling lousy seem less awful.

- *"I'm not going in there without you!"* Often vets will want to take the dog away from you to do procedures. This can be stressful for the dog.
- *"This is a scary place."* Veterinary clinics are full of strange and fearful animals, noises, people, and smells. It's no wonder many dogs want to walk out as soon as they walk in.

HOW TO SAY IT

- *Acclimate your dog to the veterinarian.* Don't wait for your dog to be ill or injured to take him to the vet. Drop by and have him weighed, or just take him in and ask the receptionist to give him a treat. If the waiting room is empty, sit there and give your dog treats. Try to give him pleasant associations with the animal hospital.
- *Choose your veterinarian carefully.* Interview potential vets and ask how they deal with anxious patients. Look for a patient and gentle vet. If your feelings toward the vet are positive, you'll have a better chance of engendering positive feelings in your dog. If the vet you like is part of a group practice, try to see him consistently, rather than the other vets, to lend stability to the experience for your dog.
- *Use lots of treats.* Take along some super-duper treats to give your dog at the vet. They can be an immense help in the waiting room to distract your dog from the other animals, and they can help improve your dog's association with the vet's office. They can also help distract your dog from a stranger's hands being all over him during an exam, although some dogs are too stressed in that situation to even take a treat.
- *Stay with your dog.* If you have a fearful dog who needs to be taken from the examination room to "the back" for procedures, ask your vet if you can go with your dog to help minimize his panic. Some vets will allow you to do this, and it can be a comfort to your dog.

- *If your vet or the vet tech wants to muzzle your dog, go ahead and do it.* It will allow the vet to do her job, it will make you less nervous, and it might even calm your dog. Work with your dog at home to acclimate him to the muzzle, using lots of treats.
- *See if you can get a house call.* Some vets operate house-call practices, where they'll come to your home to treat your pets. If your dog is very phobic about going to the vet, this might help.
- *Touch your dog at home.* Get your dog used to being touched all over her body, including her mouth. Use lots of treats, and make it fun!

HOW NOT TO SAY IT

- *Don't avoid going to the vet because your dog doesn't like it.* If you think your dog is ill or has an injury that needs veterinary attention, bite the bullet and take your dog in. As with humans, early detection is very important in many diseases. Don't let a lump, for example, become huge before a veterinarian takes a look at it.
- *Don't mask the evidence of illness.* If you're taking your dog to the vet for a specific problem, like an ear or eye infection, don't clean him up first. Your vet will want to see all the discharge and evidence of what's going on with your dog's body.

chapter twenty

Safety Hazards

Howard liked taking his American Eskimo dog, Hailey, with him when he ran errands. One day he tied Hailey to a parking meter while he dashed into the video store to get a movie. It took a few minutes longer than he expected, and when Howard came out he was horrified to see that Hailey was gone—vanished, leash and all.

Life is full of hidden dangers for our dogs. All we can do is try to minimize them. If you don't spend a few minutes in a paranoid state thinking of all that could go wrong before you try something new with your dog, you might inadvertently be putting her in harm's way. Our dogs depend upon us to keep them safe. Be diligent in avoiding hazards.

WHAT YOUR DOG IS TRYING TO TELL YOU

- *"I trust you."* Most dogs will go anywhere we ask them to and let us put them in unsafe situations. Don't violate that trust.
- *"I'm a dog."* A dog who takes the opportunity to walk off when his leash comes untied, or who bites a kid who provokes him when he's tied out in

public, or who hangs his head out the car window even though it's dangerous, is just being a dog.

- *"It's your world."* Dogs left to their own devices are pretty good about avoiding danger. But when we bring them into our world, with our unique dangers, it's up to us to keep them safe.

HOW TO SAY IT

- *Buy appropriate toys.* If your dog is an aggressive chewer, buy hardy toys. You don't want him to tear up his toys and choke, or swallow pieces and get an obstruction in his intestines. Inspect your dog's toys regularly and take away any that have been chewed down to a dangerous size. Balls should be large enough not to be accidentally swallowed. Look for any hidden hazards in toys, especially those your dog is left alone with.

- *Leave the chain collars off.* Chain collars aren't recommended by positive trainers—they don't lend themselves to positive methods. If you do use one, be sure to take it off any time you're not in a training session. Your dog could get hung up on it and choke.

- *Unplug the paper shredder.* It might sound far-fetched, but a paper shredder that turns on automatically when paper is inserted can be a real danger to your dog. Don't risk it.

- *Leave your dog at home.* Don't take your dog along on errands if you can't take her inside the store with you. Tying your dog outside the store is an invitation for trouble. Your dog could get loose and lost, someone could untie the leash, or someone could tease your dog and cause emotional trauma or provoke a bite. If you leave your dog in the car when you shop, it could get dangerously hot inside the car, even on mild days, or she could escape from the car if you leave the windows cracked. Someone could even steal your dog—or your car, with your dog in it.

- *Beware of air bags.* If your car has passenger-side air bags in the front, put your dog in the backseat. If your dog is in the front seat and the air bag is deployed, your dog could be seriously injured.

- *Use a seatbelt or other restraint.* You don't want your dog to become a missile in the event of a collision. That would be dangerous for him and for the people in the car. A variety of car restraints are available, including special harnesses, barriers, and crates. You wouldn't ride in a car without a seatbelt; don't ask your dog to.

- *Be prepared for an emergency.* Sometimes the worst-case scenario does happen, and when it does, you should be ready. (See the chapters on emergencies and on finding a lost dog for more information.)

HOW NOT TO SAY IT

- *Don't let your dog hang his head out the window of a moving car.* Sure, it's fun for him. Your child would probably like to do that, too. Would you let her? Probably not. Use the same reasoning for your dog. He could easily lose an eye to a loose piece of gravel.

- *Don't leave your dog alone in the car when it's sunny out.* The temperature in a car interior can shoot up to dangerous levels in a matter of minutes. Leave your dog at home on warm or sunny days.

- *Don't use toxic substances, like weed killers and other chemical treatments, on your lawn.* There's an alarming incidence of cancer in dogs. Although these substances might not be the reason, they are under suspicion. Why risk it?

- *Don't leave hazardous materials within reach.* Fertilizers and cleaning supplies should be kept hidden away from your dog. Antifreeze is also toxic to dogs, and dogs are attracted to its sweetness. Don't change your antifreeze near your house, and keep your dog away from shiny puddles.

- *Don't let your dog ride in the open bed of your pickup.* If he's not secured, he might fall out. If he is secured, he might fall out and hang. Even if you were able to find a truly secure way to tie him in, he's still exposed to the elements and flying pieces of gravel.

- *Don't let your dog run free.* A loose dog could be hit by a car, stolen, hurt by another animal, or even shot. An unneutered dog could be making unwanted puppies. Keep your dog in the house and make your yard escape-proof. Use a leash to give him exercise or take him to a securely fenced area.

- *Don't leave your dog in the yard while you use power equipment.* Flying sticks or pebbles could injure your dog. Plus, the noise of power tools tends to scare dogs.

chapter twenty-one

Spaying and Neutering

The night before Jim took his Mastiff, Gus, to be neutered, he started having second thoughts. *Why am I doing this?* he thought. *Gus is such a great dog. Will this change his personality? Will the recovery be difficult?* He emailed a few dog-centric friends and was reassured that any changes he saw in Gus after neutering would be positive, and that surgical recovery is quite easy.

Spaying your female dog or neutering your male is an essential component of responsible dog ownership. Unless you're participating in a well-planned breeding program (with health clearances on all the dogs being bred), there's no reason not to spay and neuter and every reason to do so. An estimated 2.5 million dogs are euthanized at shelters every year. You don't want to be part of this country's staggering pet overpopulation problem.

Knowing in advance what to expect after your dog has been spayed or neutered will help make the procedure less stressful for you and, by extension, for your dog.

WHAT YOUR DOG IS TRYING TO TELL YOU

- *"It's time."* If your young male dog starts displaying aggressive behavior, starts humping, or becomes a backyard Houdini, it's time to get him neutered. Better yet, neuter him before he starts displaying unwanted behavior.

- *"I'm uncomfortable."* Your dog will want to lick his or her incision after neutering or spaying. This is natural, but should be discouraged if the licking creates irritation or your dog starts pulling at the stitches.
- *"Ouch!"* If your dog is in post-surgical pain, try a homeopathic remedy or talk with your vet about pain medication. Don't let your dog suffer.

HOW TO SAY IT

- *Try some Arnica.* Homeopathic Arnica Montana is good for post-surgical pain. You can safely give the 30c potency (available at most health-food stores) every couple hours while your dog is in pain. Dissolve a few pellets in a tablespoon or two of water and either let your dog lap it up or put a dropperful into the side of her mouth.
- *Keep an eye on the incision.* Examine the incision at least once a day for swelling, redness, or missing stitches. Call your vet if you see anything that worries you.
- *Smell the incision.* Your nose can be a good detector of infection. If you pick up on the distinctive smell of infection, call your vet.
- *Discourage excessive licking.* If your dog is licking like mad and disturbing the wound, gently distract her from her task. Don't be harsh or punitive—after all, she's just trying to take care of herself. A stuffed Kong can be a nice way to divert her attention.
- *Try calendula ointment.* If your dog is licking a lot at his or her incision, gently dab some calendula ointment onto it. Available at health-food stores, calendula is a natural antibiotic. It won't harm your dog if he licks it, and it will help stop infection from setting in. It should also soothe itching.
- *Have your vet look at the stitches.* Even if the stitches are supposed to be dissolvable, make sure your vet takes a look at the incision after a couple weeks have passed. He or she can remove any that haven't dissolved.

Spaying and Neutering

Why should you spay or neuter your dog?

- *To avoid being part of the pet overpopulation problem.* Thousands of dogs are killed every single day in our nation's shelters. Unless you're part of a responsible breeding program designed to further your breed, there's no reason to bring more puppies into the world. Any puppies that you breed will take away homes from those who need them.
- *Because breeding is not for the faint of heart.* Breeding, done correctly, is time-consuming, expensive, and sometimes difficult.
- *It's healthy for the animal.* Spaying and neutering eliminates the chance of uterine and testicular cancers and reduces the chance of mammary and prostate cancers. Plus, a neutered male is less likely to get into fights with other dogs.

- *Try not to worry.* If you're stressed by your dog's surgery, your dog will pick up on it. Be upbeat when you leave your dog at the vet hospital.

HOW NOT TO SAY IT

- *Don't let your dog overdo it.* Follow your vet's advice about resting your dog after the surgery. He'll still be groggy when you bring him home, but he might be raring to go the next day. If your vet wants you to keep him quiet for fear of pulling out his stitches or straining them, give him quiet things to do, like licking on a stuffed Kong, and keep his exercise restricted to leash walks. (This goes for spayed females, too.)
- *If your dog is in pain (pacing, unable to get comfortable, crying out), don't let her suffer.* Either try homeopathic pain relief, like Arnica (detailed on page 78), or call your vet about prescription or over-the-counter pain medication.

- *Don't delay in spaying or neutering.* Sooner is better than later. If you spay your female before her first heat, you'll practically eliminate the chance she'll develop breast cancer. The rate of breast cancer for unspayed dogs is three times that of humans—26 percent. By spaying your dog before her first heat, you reduce that risk to 0.5 percent.
- *Don't wait for a litter.* The notion that a female should have a litter before being spayed is a myth. There's no benefit to it and, in fact, it's detrimental to her health. The more times she goes through heat early in life, the greater her chance for breast cancer.

chapter twenty-two

Vaccinations

The ritual of annual vaccinations is one that most responsible pet owners are familiar with. But more and more veterinarians—and dog owners—are starting to question the necessity and even the safety of annual revaccination. Clinical evidence doesn't exist to support the need for shots every year. And a connection is suspected between the practice of annual vaccination and life-threatening autoimmune diseases in dogs. Some veterinary schools and the American Animal Hospital Association have changed their guidelines to recommend shots every three years after initial puppy shots. Most holistic vets suggest minimal vaccinations, such as no more than a selected series of puppy shots, except rabies as required by law.

WHAT YOUR DOG IS TRYING TO TELL YOU

- *"It might not look like it, but my body's reacting poorly."* An adverse reaction to a vaccination might not happen immediately after the shot and, therefore, might not be recorded or even associated with the shot. But those shots, year after year, can have a cumulative effect.

- *"Don't give me a shot if I'm not feeling well."* Vaccines are labeled to be used on healthy dogs only.

- *"I'm old. I don't need any more shots."* Some veterinarians contend that a single shot can afford a dog many years—even a lifetime—of protection. An elderly dog who has had a lifetime of annual shots almost certainly doesn't need more, and the shot will likely be more harmful to the dog than it was when he was younger.

HOW TO SAY IT

- *Talk to your vet about titers rather than another shot.* A titer is a blood test that measures the antibodies against a specific disease that are circulating in the bloodstream at the time of the test. If sufficient antibodies are measured, it suggests that your dog is protected. The trouble with titers is that they might tell you your dog is not protected even if he is. The antibodies need not be circulating in the blood in order for them to be present and kick in when exposed to the disease. But an adequate titer can give you great peace of mind if you elect not to revaccinate.

- *Separate the shots.* If you do choose to vaccinate your dog, don't overload her system with a combination shot that protects against several different diseases. Instead, ask your vet to give a shot for a single disease (say, distemper), then come back in two weeks for the next shot (rabies or parvo). Give shots only for those diseases that are clinically significant, like distemper, parvo, and rabies.

- *Get an annual exam.* Even if your dog doesn't need to get shots, he does need to see the veterinarian at least once a year. These wellness exams can help detect early signs of disease, give you an opportunity to ask questions, and help acclimate your dog to vet visits.

HOW NOT TO SAY IT

- *Don't vaccinate if your dog is ill.* If you take your dog to the vet because he's not feeling 100 percent, resist the urge to get a booster to avoid another office visit. Shots aren't harmless—they provide a jolt to the immune system. If your dog's immune system is compromised by illness, that jolt could be harmful. The vaccine label itself stipulates that the shot is to be administered to healthy dogs only.

- *Don't vaccinate blindly.* By all means, take your dog to the vet when you get that postcard saying he's due for his annual exam. But don't automatically get the shots. Instead, talk with your vet about whether your dog really needs another vaccination. Do some research before you go to the vet, to familiarize yourself with the issue. By vaccinating judiciously, you could be saving your dog from serious illness down the road. (See the appendix for books on the vaccine controversy.)

- *Don't vaccinate unnecessarily.* Many vets choose to give combination shots for the sake of simplicity. But does your dog really need every component of the shot? Talk with your vet about which diseases your dog might need protection against and don't give him shots for any others. Remember, vaccinations aren't harmless. They contain adjuvants, such as aluminum hydroxide, designed to stimulate a longer immune response. Do you want to introduce these foreign substances unnecessarily?

- *Don't combine vaccinations with other stressful procedures.* If your dog is at the vet for a spay or neuter surgery, don't stress her body further by giving her a vaccination at the same time. Same goes for any procedure, like dental cleaning or X rays, for which anesthesia is necessary.

part three

Communicating Through Training

Training opens the lines of communication with your dog and creates a common language. It's a great way to spend quality time with your dog. Most of all, it should be fun for both you and your dog. Your smile and laughter are both important ways to communicate while you're training.

Positive training is based on a very simple principle: Dogs (and all other beings, for that matter) will repeat behaviors that are reinforced. They don't repeat behaviors that aren't reinforced. So catch your dog doing something right and reward her for it. If she does something you don't like, just ignore it. Give her something else to do. If you set your dog up for success and minimize opportunities for your dog to get into trouble, you'll find that you have lots to reinforce and little to ignore.

chapter twenty-three

Crate Training

Lucy, a Labrador Retriever, acts like a maniac in her crate. As soon as the door is closed, she howls and paws at the door and acts as if she were being put into solitary confinement forever. Her owner, Michael, feels terrible every time he puts her in there at night, but he knows that if he doesn't, he'll wake up to destroyed furniture.

A crate (a plastic or wire cage) can be a terrific training tool. Some dogs take to their crate like a fish to water, while others appear to regard it as a prison. By helping your dog enjoy his crate—and perhaps asking him to spend less time there—you can make the crate the safe haven it should be.

WHAT YOUR DOG IS TRYING TO TELL YOU

- *"Let me out of here!!"* Your dog might bark and carry on because he doesn't want to be in the crate. If you let him out as he's barking, you'll reinforce that behavior.
- *"I want to be with you!"* Most dogs don't like to be isolated from their families. If you're at home, yet feel the need to crate your dog, at least keep her in the room with you.

- *"I have to go to the bathroom."* Dogs instinctively don't like to soil their den, so they don't want to go to the bathroom in their crate. This makes it a great tool for housetraining. But if your dog is left in there too long (beyond the capacity of his bladder), it becomes a torture chamber.

- *"I'm bored in here!"* A crate can be a boring place if there's nothing inside but a dog. But you can stock the crate with goodies that will help keep your dog occupied until he's ready for a nap.

- *"I spend too much time in here."* It's not fair to crate your dog day and night. If you crate him during the day, be sure he gets plenty of free time to interact with you at night.

HOW TO SAY IT

- *Introduce the crate positively.* Entice your dog into the crate by tossing treats into it. When she sticks her head in toward the treat, click and let her get the treat. Gradually toss the treats farther and farther into the crate until she willingly goes into the crate and stays in it while you give her treats. Close the door briefly, click and treat for quiet behavior, then gradually extend the time the door is closed.

- *Let your dog try the crate on his own.* Leave the crate accessible to your dog when you're home so he can go in and out at will. Plant tasty surprises in the crate to make it more interesting to him. Better yet, feed him in his crate. Praise him whenever you see him go in his crate, and be nonchalant when he leaves the crate.

- *Make the crate a special place.* When you put your dog in her crate, give her something delicious to chew on. Take a safe, hollow toy, like a Kong, stuff it with kibble, treats, or biscuits, and seal it up with peanut butter or cream cheese. To make it last an especially long time, freeze it. By the time your dog finishes licking out all the goodies, she'll be tired and ready for a nap.

- *Try a different kind of crate.* If your dog really dislikes the crate you've provided, try an alternate kind. For example, some dogs like the denlike atmosphere of a plastic, Vari-Kennel–type crate (the kind airlines accept). Others want to be part of the action and prefer the visibility of the wire type. If you can, borrow a crate from a friend before investing in one, so that you can more affordably switch types if necessary.

- *Try some Rescue Remedy.* If your dog is stressed when he's left in his crate, try giving him a few drops of the Bach Rescue Remedy flower essence, which can be effective at relieving stress. Simply put a few drops in his water, on his tongue, or even rub it into his ears.

- *Use the crate when you're home.* The crate can be a great holding place for when you need your dog to be out of the way temporarily (like when a repair person is in the house). It can also be used for a humane time-out. Your dog should get used to going in the crate when you're at home for times like these.

- *Work toward not relying on the crate.* If your dog is housetrained and doesn't chew up the house, she shouldn't need to be in a crate when you're not at home. If you suspect she's now reliable, leave her loose in the house for a short period of time. Then gradually lengthen the time until you know you can trust her.

- *Think about alternatives.* If your dog is really stressed by the crate but has destructive tendencies, leave him loose in part of the house and dog-proof that part. Don't turn his crate into a prison.

- *Make the crate a safe place.* If you have kids, instruct them not to disturb the dog when she's in her crate. Explain that it's her room and as such is her private place. Your dog should look to her crate as a place where she can get away from the hustle and bustle of the family if she wants to.

HOW NOT TO SAY IT

- *Don't punish your dog by angrily forcing him into his crate.* If your dog does something wrong and you throw him into the crate with nothing to do, he'll develop lifelong negative associations with it. If your dog likes his crate, though, a time-out in the crate with a stuffed Kong—and no yelling from you—can be a good way to take him out of a situation if he's misbehaving.

- *Don't abuse the crate.* Don't leave your dog in her crate for hours on end. Keeping an adult dog in a crate during the workday can be a short-term solution to the problem of a destructive dog. But the dog should be trained to be reliable—or confined to larger spaces—so she doesn't end up spending half her life in a small space. Some working people will crate their dogs during the day, come home and let them out to pee and eat, then put them right back in while they go out for the evening. That's no way for a dog to live. A dog kept like this has every reason to believe her crate is a prison, rather than a haven.

- *Don't keep a puppy in a crate all day.* Their little bladders can't handle it. If you leave a puppy in his crate so long that he's forced to pee and sit in the mess, you've ruined the crate as a housetraining tool. And you've given your puppy a very bad day. If you must leave your puppy all day, put him in a bathroom or other room with newspapers or potty pads during the day. Leave the crate—with the door open—in the room with the puppy. (See the chapter on housetraining.)

- *Don't let your dog out of the crate if she fusses.* If it's time to let your dog out, wait until she quiets down before you reward her by opening the crate door. If you open it while she's barking, you reward the barking. Instead, wait for a few seconds of quiet, then open the door.

- *Do not bang on the top of the crate to get your dog to be quiet.* Can you imagine how loud and frightening banging on the crate must sound to a dog? It might stop him from barking, but it will also make his crate a scary place.

- *Don't buy a crate that's too big or too small.* Your dog's crate should be just big enough for her to stand up, turn around, and lie down comfortably. Too big and it becomes useless as a housetraining tool. Too small and it's uninviting. If you want to buy a crate for your large-breed puppy that will last her lifetime, you can block one end with something, like a concrete block, to make a large crate smaller while she's a puppy.

chapter twenty-four

Housetraining

Amy felt that her dog, Otis, was about 90 percent housetrained. He knew to go to the bathroom outside and he always pottied when taken out. Amy never caught Otis in the act, yet occasionally, she'd find unpleasant surprises in the house. Just when she thought housetraining was behind her, she'd find another puddle. She started worrying that she'd never be able to trust her dog!

Housetraining mistakes are not uncommon, if dogs are given the opportunity to make them. Living with a dog who is not fully housetrained can be frustrating, not to mention embarrassing when friends enter a smelly home. But most dogs can be housetrained if the owner is consistent and attentive.

WHAT YOUR DOG IS TRYING TO TELL YOU

- *"Teach me where you want me to relieve myself."* Puppies aren't born with the knowledge that they should eliminate outside. It's up to you to teach your pup—by taking her where you want her to potty and rewarding her.

- *"I don't know what I'm supposed to do."* You think your dog is housetrained? Maybe not. If your dog still doesn't get it, he might see nothing wrong with relieving himself on the carpet.

- *"I can't help it."* There might be a medical explanation for your dog's inability to hold her urine or feces until you let her out. If your dog has been completely housetrained but starts making mistakes, have her checked out by a vet.

- *"I gotta go!"* Some dogs, particularly small ones, have tiny bladders and simply can't hold it as long as you'd like them to. In that instance, you need to figure out a way for your dog to get out at the interval she needs, or provide a place indoors where she can be permitted to relieve herself.

- *"It's cold out there!"* On inclement days, going outside to potty might be unattractive to some dogs. It's up to you to make pottying outside more attractive during the training process, by giving your dog treats and praise when he goes where you want him to.

- *"You intimidate me."* Submissive urination happens when a shy dog wants to show a person that she is submissive to them. It isn't a housetraining problem, per se. (See the chapter on submissive urination for more information on handling this problem.)

- *"This is my house, and I'm the big man here."* Some dogs, particularly male dogs, will lift their leg inside the house to mark their territory. (See the chapter on marking for more information.)

HOW TO SAY IT

- *Reward her for going potty outside.* Always go outside with your dog until she is fully housetrained. Then, when she does her business outside, praise her and give her a treat. Don't wait until she's come back inside to give her the treat, or you'll be rewarding her coming in, not pottying. In order to keep on top of her housetraining, you must go outside with her so you know for a fact that she's gone to the bathroom.

- *Use an enzymatic cleaner.* Clean the mess with a cleaner designed specifically for pet stains and odors that contains enzymes. These cleaners eliminate the odor, rather than just masking it. Dogs tend to want to pee where they (or another dog) have peed before. Their noses are so sensitive that unless the odor is completely eliminated, they'll still pick up on it, even if we can't smell it. Using an enzymatic cleaner can help you avoid repeat mistakes in the same spot.

- *Keep an eye on your dog.* If your dog starts to go to the bathroom in front of you in the house, unemotionally hustle him outside. When he finishes the job outside, give him a treat. If your dog potties in the house, out of sight, there's nothing you can do about it.

- *Use a long-term confinement area when you're away.* You can't ask a young dog to go all day without eliminating. If you have to spend the day away from your puppy (or an adult who is not fully housetrained), confine her in an easy-to-clean room, like a bathroom, with her crate (with the door open), her chew toys, and her water bowl. Designate a place—on the opposite corner of the room from her bed—that she can use for a toilet. Veterinary behaviorist Ian Dunbar recommends using the same material for the toilet that you want your dog to use outdoors: for example, a piece of sod, if your dog will eliminate primarily on grass, or a thin concrete slab if she'll use the sidewalk. You're helping your puppy develop a preference for the right place to eliminate.

- *Crate your dog.* If you can't keep an eye on your dog when you're at home, put him in his crate. Most dogs will not go to the bathroom in their crate, because that violates their built-in tendency to keep their den clean. A word of caution: Don't crate your dog for extended periods of time. It's not fair to ask him to hold it longer than is comfortable. Use a long-term confine ment area instead. When you let your dog out of the crate, take him right outside to go to the bathroom. (See the chapter on crate training for more information on using a crate.)

- *Try a tether.* Keep your dog tethered to you when you're home and neither you nor your dog is sleeping. This "umbilical cord" method will facilitate bonding between the two of you and ensure that your dog cannot make mistakes in the house when you're not looking. Take her out frequently during the day, particularly after she eats or gets up from a nap.

- *Keep a schedule.* Put your dog on a strict food and water schedule so you have a better idea of when he will have to go to the bathroom. Then be sure to let him out during those times and reward him for doing his business outside. That way he learns that when he potties outside, he gets relief and a tasty treat. Pottying inside (in the long-term confinement area) only gives relief.
- *See the vet.* There might be a medical explanation for your dog's housetraining mistakes.
- *Teach her to do it on cue.* While your dog is going to the bathroom outside, use a word or phrase like "Go potty" or "Hurry up." Then, after your dog has associated that cue with the act, you'll be able to use it to get him to go potty outside. Very handy on a rainy day!
- *Try a litter box or pads.* If your dog is small, you might want to purchase a doggy litter box, sold under the name Second Nature. Of course, it'll be your responsibility to keep the litter box clean. Another option are superabsorbent housebreaking pads you can leave out for your dog to use. The pads are treated with pheromones to entice your dog to use them.

HOW NOT TO SAY IT

- *Never punish your dog for going to the bathroom in the house.* You'll just give him a reason not to potty in front of you. The result? A stealth pooper or one who might not even want to relieve himself outside in front of you. The old advice about rubbing a dog's nose in his mistake is abusive, period.
- *Don't mess with the routine.* If you're expecting your (adult) dog to hold it all day when you're at work, come home from work close to the same time every day. Dogs thrive on routine, and that routine is never more important than when you're dealing with housetraining.
- *Don't give your dog the run of the house.* If your dog is not 100 percent housetrained, confine her to easy-to-clean rooms until you can trust her. Gradually increase, room by room, the amount of freedom she gets.

Dog Talk

Housetraining

Housetraining mistakes can be caused by a health problem. If an already housetrained dog starts to make mistakes in the house, a visit to the vet is in order. Even an unhousetrained adult or a puppy should see the vet if the housetraining is particularly challenging, just to rule out a medical cause. A host of medical problems can cause your dog to have accidents in the house, including urinary tract infection, hormonal imbalance (spayed females, in particular, can start to leak due to a lack of estrogen in their system), diabetes, tumors, and gastrointestinal upset.

- *Don't expect too much.* A little puppy can't hold it all day. Don't ask him to. Either leave him in a long-term confinement that's easy to clean up (and expect him to go potty inside in your absence), or crate him when you're not home, but arrange for a midday potty break. If your dog is already housetrained, a dog door can give him access to the fenced yard at all times.
- *Don't stay in the house when your dog goes outside.* If you're still working on housetraining, you need to be in the yard with your dog so you can reward her for pottying outside and so you know for a fact she's done so.

chapter twenty-five

Meeting New Dogs

Taylor's Cairn Terrier, Squirt, is unpredictable around new dogs. Sometimes she gets along fine with them; other times introductions turn into a snarl fest. To her human's embarrassment, Squirt has been known to growl and lunge at other dogs, seemingly without provocation.

Not unlike people, dogs have different reactions to new dogs, and their reactions change, depending on the dog they're being introduced to. Much of the behavior is rooted in fear. But the humans can go a long way toward making introductions, be they to new dogs in the family or just potential new friends, go more smoothly.

WHAT YOUR DOG IS TRYING TO TELL YOU

- *"I'm afraid."* A dog who snarls at a new dog is often showing fear. He might be afraid that the other dog will hurt him or afraid because he's on-leash and has no flight path. Or he might think you're afraid, which makes him afraid, too.
- *"Wanna play?"* Some dogs greet new dogs with play bows and spins in an effort to get a play session started.

- *"Knock it off."* If your dog meets a new dog who's in his face (perhaps just out of pushy overexuberance), your dog might growl a warning to try to get him to behave more politely.
- *"At last! Another dog!"* If your dog is usually deprived of canine company, he might be so enthusiastic about seeing another dog that he's in that dog's face and too enthusiastic. This might make the other dog unhappy.
- *"Let's see who's boss."* When a pair of confident dogs meet, there might be some jockeying for the role of king of the group.
- *"I mean no harm."* Some dogs who feel threatened by a new dog will use calming signals or more overt body language to let the new dog know they're not a threat.

HOW TO SAY IT

- *Stay relaxed and upbeat.* If your dog is meeting a new dog on-leash, keep the leash loose. Keep breathing. Your dog will take his cue from you: If you're tense, he'll be tense. If you're afraid of how your dog is going to react to the new dog, you'll transfer your fears to him. So take a deep breath (then let it out) and don't tighten up that leash.
- *Try to make the introductions off-leash.* If you're in a safe area, take off your dog's leash before meeting a new dog. Dogs are much more relaxed when they're able to walk away from a situation. And without the hindrance of a leash, they can approach from the side, a common calming signal. Of course, if this meeting is taking place on a city sidewalk, the safety of the leash is more important than the relaxation benefits of being off-leash.
- *Watch the calming signals.* Once you're familiar with calming signals, it's fascinating to watch for them. Dogs use them all the time when they're meeting new dogs, particularly when they're off-leash. See how many you can identify: Look for the sideways approach, ground sniffing, yawning, and averted eyes.
- *Walk with the new dog.* If you're meeting a friend and her dog on a walk, after a brief greeting period, walk the two dogs together, side by side. Even

if they're inclined to be adversarial, the fact that they're not facing one another can lessen the tension.

- *Remember that there's no right or wrong.* We all like our dogs to be likeable, but if your dog reacts to another dog in a negative way, it's not a reflection on either dog. Don't be embarrassed if your dog snarls or acts aloof. He's just being who he is.

HOW NOT TO SAY IT

- *Don't feel like your dog has to greet every dog you see.* If your dog isn't into new dogs, or can't seem to be introduced to one without a fracas ensuing, don't have him meet every new dog in sight. If you see another dog coming your way, it's perfectly acceptable to either cross the street or walk by the other dog without a meet-and-greet. You can help your dog become comfortable with new dogs under more structured conditions with the help of a trainer.

- *Don't think the worst.* When your dog approaches a new dog, visualize success, not failure. It's easy for your mind to jump to a worst-case scenario, but by visualizing a pleasant greeting, you'll help yourself relax—and perhaps your dog will, too.

- *Don't overreact.* Don't yank your dog away as soon as one dog lifts a lip. Get to know your dog, his reactions, and his body language. If he's truly uncomfortable with another dog, just calmly walk him away. But if he and the other dog are merely posturing to establish some ground rules, that might be all that's necessary for them to form a relationship that will last for years.

- *Don't let your dog bound up to other dogs without permission.* If you see another dog, ask the person at the other end of the leash whether it is okay for the dogs to greet one another. Some dogs can be very grumpy with new dogs.

chapter twenty-six

Selecting a Trainer

Debbie's Wheaten Terrier puppy, Arlo, is a cute, fiery bundle of energy and love. As he approaches adolescence, she realizes that she'd be wise to get him into a class. She can use some help in channeling Arlo's energy, teaching him good manners, and making him easier to live with. But she doesn't know how to go about finding a good trainer who will help solve, rather than create, problems with her pup.

Selecting a trainer is an extremely important decision. You'll want to find someone who will offer advice that you can use for the lifetime of your dog. You'll want one who uses effective methods—but those methods need to be humane. Asking some important questions and observing a class in advance can help you find a positive, humane trainer who will become a friend to both you and your dog.

WHAT YOUR DOG IS TRYING TO TELL YOU

- *"Let's make it fun!"* You'll want to eagerly anticipate, not dread, your training classes. Your dog should enjoy the classes, too.

- *"Don't be harsh with me."* Traditional, correction-based training programs use aversives to tell your dog what not to do. Positive-reinforcement-based programs use rewards to show your dog what you want him to do. Which do you think your dog would prefer?

HOW TO SAY IT

- *Ask around.* Watch the relationship between your friends and their dogs. Look for those whose dogs aren't making them tear their hair out, then ask them what trainer they used. Your veterinarian might be able to recommend a trainer, but be sure to specify that you're looking for a trainer who uses positive methods. Listen for the same name to come up repeatedly. Ask about the trainers' methods and what the people liked and didn't like about them.

- *Do some research.* Before you contact a trainer, know what you're looking for. The tenets of this book are based on progressive, positively focused training methods. To find a trainer who uses those methods, contact the Association of Pet Dog Trainers (APDT), a trainers' organization that promotes positive training (see the appendix for contact information). You can learn about APDT members in your area and read guidelines on what to look for in a positive trainer at the APDT website.

- *Look for a certified trainer.* The APDT has developed a pet dog trainer certification program—which is being implemented by the Certification Council for Pet Dog Trainers—that requires certified trainers to pass a rigorous test of their knowledge of positive training methods and animal behavior. Trainers must have 300 hours of training experience before taking the test. Trainers who pass the test are allowed to use the initials CPDT after their name. The program is new and there aren't many certified trainers yet, so the absence of CPDT isn't necessarily significant. But if you see the initials after someone's name, you'll know the trainer is knowledgeable, experienced, and well versed in positive methods.

- *Call some trainers.* Talk to trainers who have been recommended to you and ask them about their training methods. Listen for phrases like "clicker training" or "lure and reward." Tell them about your specific problems with your dog and see how comfortable you are with their responses. Find out what kind of collars they recommend—positive trainers won't have you putting a choke chain on your dog. Find out about their experience and credentials. How long has she (or he) been training? How long has she used her current methods? The best trainers continue to go to seminars to keep up on the newest theories and methods.

- *Visit a class.* A reputable trainer will allow you to sit in on a class (without your dog) before signing up for one. Watch the way the trainer interacts with the students, both human and canine. Gauge the level of enjoyment in the class. Is everyone having fun? Close your eyes and listen: Is there a lot of happy talk and praise? Or do you hear shouting and frustration?
- *Trust your instincts.* If a trainer's methods make you uncomfortable, don't sign up for the class. If you're already in the class and you're asked to do something to your dog that you hesitate to do, listen to your gut. Don't do it. Leave the class if you have to. It's easy for harsh methods to damage your relationship with your dog. You don't want that to happen.
- *Listen to your dog.* When you go to a class, watch your dog's reactions. His behavior should improve through the weeks of the class, not degrade.

HOW NOT TO SAY IT

- *Price and convenience shouldn't be the priority in choosing a trainer.* Their training methods should be the number-one consideration.
- *Don't do anything that makes you uncomfortable.* If a trainer asks you to do something that just doesn't feel right, don't do it. They might be the authority, but you know your dog. Your relationship with your dog is very important, and you don't want to damage it.
- *Don't hesitate to drop a class.* If you end up choosing the wrong trainer for you, don't worry about dropping the class. If you find that your trainer is becoming frustrated with you or your dog, you may have tested the limits of her experience. Look around for a better situation so your dog gets the benefit of the training. Don't stick with a bad situation for the sake of not being a quitter. Forfeit the class fee if you have to.

chapter twenty-seven

Teaching "Leave It"

Monte is a cute young Spaniel mix with a little bit of the devil in him. The imp strolls around the house, looking for things to get into. Once—right in front of his mom's nose—he actually stole money out of her wallet and chewed it up!

If you teach your dog to "leave it"—that is, to step away from whatever he's touching or paying attention to—you'll find it comes in handy. A simple "Leave it" from his mom could have stopped Monte from eating that money. Garbage hounds can be stopped before the trash reaches their lips. It's not hard to teach "Leave it," and teaching it can even be fun.

WHAT YOUR DOG IS TRYING TO TELL YOU

- *"What's this?"* Dogs explore with their noses and mouths. Unfortunately, they don't always have good judgment when it comes to deciding what's appropriate to pick up or eat.
- *"Eat first, ask questions later."* Some dogs will ingest anything they come across, edible or not.

- *"I want it!"* Dogs will grab things and try to chew them up or stash them away. Using "Leave it" can help you prevent a game of keep-away or tug over the item.

HOW TO SAY IT

- *Play "doggie zen."* Operating under the zen principle that you must give up something in order to get it, doggie zen is a fun game that dogs catch on to quickly. Put an aromatic treat in your closed fist and hold it in front of your dog's nose. He'll sniff at it, try to bite at it, maybe even paw at it. Just ignore these efforts and keep your fist closed. Eventually, out of frustration if nothing else, he'll pull his nose away from your fist. Be ready to click, then give him the treat. Try this a few times, and before long you'll see that he pulls back after a single sniff. At this point, add the cue "Leave it" after you offer the closed fist.

- *Move it to the floor.* After your dog has mastered doggie zen, try putting the treat on the floor in front of her. She'll go for it, but gently tell her "Leave it" and cover the treat with your hand or foot if you have to, or step between your dog and the item. When she backs away, click and give her a different treat (so she doesn't learn that it's okay to pick up forbidden items from the floor). Try this with toys or any other coveted item.

- *Pay attention to your dog.* You can't tell your dog to leave it if you're not watching her. If you have an exuberant dog who tends to get into trouble in the house, keep her with you (or nearby) so you can supervise. Give her sanctioned things to chew on.

HOW NOT TO SAY IT

- *Don't holler "LEAVE IT!" when your dog is going for an item.* Life's much more pleasant if you can calmly tell her to leave it and she does. Hollering at your dog can damage your relationship and isn't necessary. Save yelling for emergencies.

- *Don't leave valuable items around for your dog to put his mouth on.* Then you won't need "Leave it" as often.

part four

A Positive Approach to Specific Behavior Challenges

No dog is perfect. If you have a problem or two with your dog, you may have tried yelling or punishing—and you've probably noticed it doesn't have a lasting effect. Many problems can be addressed by either management (taking away the opportunity for your dog to misbehave) or redirecting your dog to an alternative behavior. By reinforcing the behavior you want and making it difficult for your dog to perform the behavior you don't like, the problem behavior tends to disappear. It's easy to unwittingly reward unwanted behavior, so look at the problem through your dog's eyes. How is the behavior rewarding to your dog?

Switching to positive methods might require you to change the way you think about your dog. If you're trapped in a mindset that requires you to show your dog that you're the boss or not allow the dog to get away with "bad" behavior, you miss out on opportunities to reward your dog for good behavior. Once the problem behaviors start to go away (and sometimes it takes the help of a professional trainer or behaviorist for that to happen), the barriers to your building a closer relationship with your dog will start to vanish as well.

chapter twenty-eight

Aggression with Other Dogs

When Al takes his unneutered male Akita, Dante, to the dog park, more often than not Dante gets into a fight. It doesn't appear to Al that Dante always starts the fight, but sometimes he's the attacker. Dante is starting to become a social pariah: Al notices that people leash their dogs and walk away when he and Dante approach. Al feels that Dante needs his exercise, so he doesn't want to stop taking him to the park, but he's at a loss about how to get Dante to get along better with his fellow canines.

A dog-aggressive dog is much more stressful to own than a friendly one. If your dog is aggressive toward other dogs, you must always be on the alert for approaching dogs. You can't relax when you are outside the house with your dog. Luckily, dog aggression isn't usually the death sentence that aggression toward humans often is. By avoiding harsh punishment and increasing your dog's positive exposures to other dogs, you can make him more comfortable with other dogs.

WHAT YOUR DOG IS TRYING TO TELL YOU

- *"I'm afraid!"* Many dogs will act aggressively out of fear. If your dog's afraid of another dog and can't run away, he might feel forced to lash out to defend himself against the perceived threat.
- *"I'm undersocialized."* Dogs who weren't exposed to good-natured dogs as puppies really missed out. They didn't learn how to read other dogs and often think the worst about any dog they meet.
- *"I'm not perfect."* We seem to expect dogs to never get into arguments with other dogs. What humans go through life without losing their tempers? We shouldn't ask that of a dog. We can ask that the arguments don't go beyond shouting, though.
- *"I hurt."* Your dog might be in pain and, therefore, touchy and grumpy.

HOW TO SAY IT

- *Observe the damage.* If your dog gets into fights but doesn't send other dogs to the veterinarian, he's demonstrating good bite inhibition. He might be a pain to be around, but he's probably not going to seriously hurt another dog. If, however, he severely injures any dog he fights with, the situation is more grave.
- *Look for a special class.* Some trainers offer classes, sometimes called "growl" classes, specifically for aggressive dogs. If you can find a class that uses positive methods, like classical conditioning (where your dog is given treats when other dogs are around) as well as operant conditioning (where your dog is rewarded for good behavior around other dogs), you can help your dog gain confidence and become better socialized. See if the Association of Pet Dog Trainers can help you locate such a class near you. (See the appendix for contact information.)
- *If you can't find a growl class, call a positive trainer or behaviorist and ask him or her to evaluate your dog.* Together, design a plan of careful socialization and conditioning that will allow your dog to be more comfortable around other dogs.

- *Stay calm.* It's natural for you to tense up when you see another dog if you think your dog is going to react badly. But your dog picks up on your tension, and it reinforces her belief that the other dog is something to be wary of. Keep breathing, try to stay upbeat, and walk your dog away from the other dog, clicking and treating for good behavior. A trainer can give you more information on how to handle specific situations with your dog.

- *Visualize the positive.* Don't automatically think the worst when your dog approaches (or is approached by) another dog. Instead, visualize the two sniffing and going through ordinary greeting rituals. This will keep you more relaxed, and your dog might stay more relaxed, too.

- *Neuter him.* If your dog is intact, those hormones aren't helping his aggressive tendencies. They'll not only make him more inclined to fight, they also tend to make him more of a target of other dogs. You'll both be able to relax more if your dog is neutered.

- *Get a check-up.* If your dog's aggression starts suddenly or for no apparent reason, get her to the vet for a thorough work-up to rule out a physical reason for her grumpiness. A visit to a veterinary chiropractor might help as well.

HOW NOT TO SAY IT

- *Don't punish your dog for acting aggressively.* If you yank your dog away and yell at him, you're giving him all the more reason to have negative associations with other dogs.

- *Don't isolate your dog.* If your dog's not getting along with other dogs, it's natural to completely avoid other dogs. But the aggression won't get better that way. Instead, contact a trainer or a behaviorist and seek supervised opportunities for socialization. Your dog needs to have positive interactions with other dogs.

- *Don't inhibit your dog's ability to greet other dogs.* Let your dog go through normal greeting rituals with other dogs, provided you don't see signs of violence. Pulling her away or keeping the leash tight will increase the stress of the situation.

- *Don't mistake rough play for aggression.* Many dogs sound ferocious when they're playing. But there's no need to pull them apart if both dogs are enjoying the interaction.

- *Don't freak out.* If your dog gets into a single fight, it doesn't mean he's an aggressive dog. Dogs, like humans, lose their temper when pushed. If your dog starts a fight, it might be provoked, even if you can't see the provocation. Be careful if you let your dog around that dog again, but don't limit your dog's exposure to all dogs based on a single incident.

chapter twenty-nine

Aggression with People

Rhonda thought she could trust her dog, Simba. The German Shepherd sometimes growled at people, but Rhonda never thought she'd bite. But when a boisterous visitor came into the house and reached out to pet Simba, the dog bit his hand in a flash. All of a sudden Rhonda's confidence was shaken, and she didn't know how to make sure that Simba didn't bite anyone else.

All dogs can bite. But dogs who bite people are not welcome in our society (unless they're trained attack dogs who bite only under direction). If you have a dog who bites—or one who seems like she's going to bite someone eventually—seek help immediately. Don't take any chances. If you do, you risk someone getting hurt, you risk a lawsuit, and you risk a death sentence for your dog.

WHAT YOUR DOG IS TRYING TO TELL YOU

- *"I'm afraid!"* Many aggressive dogs act out of fear. It's the old "the best defense is a good offense" strategy.
- *"I'm stressed."* If a number of stressful things happen at once, it can push a dog past his limit.

- *"Get out of my territory!"* Some dogs will attack when they're defending their territory or loved ones from a perceived threat.
- *"I hurt."* Any dog will bite if he's in pain or if someone's hurting him.
- *"I'm just playing!"* Unruly, uncontrolled dogs might bite at a human in play, just as they'd bite at a dog in play. If they've never been taught bite inhibition (see the chapter on mouthing), that bite might be painful indeed.

HOW TO SAY IT

- *Seek professional help.* If you see any problem with aggression in your dog, seek help immediately. No book can tell you how to treat your individual dog's problem. See a behaviorist with experience in treating aggression before the situation escalates and someone gets hurt. Look for one who uses positive methods, like desensitization and conditioning, combined with management, rather than one who escalates the situation with punishment and physical domination.
- *Heed warnings.* If your dog is growling at you or others, take this for the warning that your dog means it to be. Seek help from a behaviorist. Learn to distinguish between the play growling, which many dogs will do when they're playing with people and other animals, and the growl that's saying "Back off." If you can't tell the difference, a trainer or behaviorist can help you.
- *Use a muzzle.* Don't hesitate to put a muzzle on your dog when you go out of the house if she's in danger of biting someone. This management tool is not an answer to your problem, of course—a dog can't spend her life muzzled—but it will help keep people safe while you deal with the problem.

HOW NOT TO SAY IT

- *Don't tackle the problem on your own.* Aggression has serious, life-altering consequences. Don't endanger other people (or yourself)—seek help from a qualified professional.

- *Don't physically punish your dog for aggression.* If you manhandle your dog because he's threatening you, you're asking to get hurt. And you're doing nothing to help your dog's aggression problems.
- *Don't foist your problem on others.* If your dog's aggression problem can be solved with the help of a behaviorist, perhaps finding a new home with someone who can devote the time and resources to turning the dog around would work, assuming you can't. But if your dog's problem is severe, it's not fair to put someone in danger by placing her elsewhere. If you do look for a new home for your aggressive dog, you must fully disclose your dog's problems to prospective adopters or shelters.
- *Don't rule out euthanasia.* If a behaviorist (or, better, more than one behaviorist) evaluates your dog and says he can't be rehabilitated, euthanasia might be the most humane option. It could be a better alternative for your dog than spending a lifetime in isolation.

chapter thirty

Excessive Barking

Chris's Sheltie, Leroy, barks frenetically at the slightest provocation—if he looks out the window and sees even a leaf blowing in the lawn, he'll go into a barking frenzy. Playing a game of chase with the kids creates a huge commotion. Some days Chris wishes that Leroy would just shut up and take a nap.

Some dogs bark a lot. They do so for a variety of reasons, all of which they consider perfectly legitimate. Sometimes that bark can be truly useful, for instance if the dog is warning against something important. You wouldn't really want a mute dog who didn't tell you about someone trying to break in, would you? But when the dog is simply barking at evil nothings, it can make you want to tear your hair out.

Luckily, dogs can be trained to limit their barking. By using some simple, positive steps—and by not putting your dog into a position where he feels compelled to bark excessively—you can help make your dog a quiet companion.

WHAT YOUR DOG IS TRYING TO TELL YOU

- *"Stay away!"* Dogs will use their voices to deter people from entering your house or yard. This is a perfectly legitimate reason for a dog to bark.

- *"There's someone at the door!"* A ringing doorbell almost always means someone's going to come into the house, or at the very least, interact with someone in the house. That's something most dogs consider cause for barking—they've got to let you know someone's there.

- *"Don't leave me!"* Some dogs are very vocal about their displeasure at being left home alone.

- *"I'm bored!"* Outdoor dogs will entertain themselves by barking hours on end out of sheer boredom. Indoor dogs do it sometimes, too.

- *"I'm lonely."* Dogs are pack animals and like to be with their families. Being relegated to the yard when everyone else is inside or being left alone for hours on end can cause a dog to bark in protest.

HOW TO SAY IT

- *Interrupt your dog's barking, but in a positive way.* When your dog starts to bark, call his name. When he turns to look at you, click and treat. This interruption should stop the barking, and when he's quiet for a moment say "Quiet [or Shhhh], good dog!" and click again. Then give him a treat. You're creating a pleasant diversion for your dog, and he will soon associate "Quiet" or "Shhhh" with the state of being quiet.

- *Take away the stimulus.* If you can figure out what sets your dog off, try to limit her access to it. For example, close the window shade or block the window so she can't see out.

- *Bring your dog inside.* If your dog is barking in the yard, just bring him in. He can't bother your neighbors if he's not outside to bark. He'll be less lonely and, therefore, less inclined to bark. He'll be less bored, because there's more going on indoors. And if you're home, you can ask him to be quiet.

- *Look to see what your dog's barking about.* It could be something important! If it is, do something about the problem and praise your dog profusely. If not, interrupt his barking and reward the quiet. And bring him inside if he's in the yard.

- *Turn on some music.* Before you leave the house, turn on the radio or the television to keep your dog company and help muffle exterior noises that might prompt her to bark.

- *Provide plenty of exercise and stimulation.* If your dog's asleep or otherwise occupied, he'll be less likely to bark at the slightest provocation. Make sure he gets plenty of exercise on a daily basis. Give him interactive toys that you fill with food or treats. Your dog will spend many happy minutes or even hours trying to figure out how to get the toy to release the treats. Another way to keep him occupied is to give him a hollow rubber Kong toy filled with treats and plugged with peanut butter or cream cheese. He'll lick and lick to get it all out. Then, with any luck, he'll go to sleep.

HOW NOT TO SAY IT

- *Don't holler "QUIET!!!" when your dog barks.* Your dog will think you're simply joining her in a chorus of barking, and screaming at your dog isn't good for your relationship.

- *Don't soothingly calm your dog with petting to get him to stop barking.* This rewards his barking, rather than rewarding him for being quiet. Rather, pet him after he's stopped barking and immediately stop if he starts barking again.

- *Don't use an anti-barking shock collar.* It's not fair to punish your dog by making a natural function, like barking, painful. If you're pushed to the limit and an anti-barking collar will keep you from being evicted, use a citronella collar that punishes your dog with an unpleasant smell, rather than an electric shock.

- *Don't debark your dog.* Taking away a dog's voice is like taking away a human's. It's cruel, plain and simple. Besides, even with the vocal chords cut, a dog still barks, it's just a raspy whisper rather than a full-blown bark.

- *Don't blame the dog for barking, especially if your dog belongs to one of the breeds known to be barkers.* This includes many of the herding breeds, some toy dogs, and some Terriers. Doing your homework prior to acquiring a dog can help you avoid insistent barkers. If you know your nerves (or those of your neighbors) are easily frazzled, look into getting a calmer breed next time around. (See the appendix for books that help in choosing a breed.)

chapter thirty-one

Bolting out the Door

Little Fritz is like greased lightning when the door opens. Before his owner, Charlie, can grab him, the Jack Russell Terrier is outside and running down the street. So far he hasn't been hurt, but this habit is a tragedy waiting to happen.

Bolting out an open door is a dangerous habit that should be stopped immediately. You can train your dog to wait at the door. Until he's trained well, however, you mustn't give your dog the opportunity to bolt.

WHAT YOUR DOG IS TRYING TO TELL YOU

- *"Freedom!"* It's fun to get out and explore the neighborhood. Dogs with a high prey drive might take off at the sight of a small animal—or just at the possibility of chasing a small animal.
- *"Catch me if you can!"* Keep-away is another game dogs love. What better way to get Mom or Dad to run after you than to run out the door?
- *"Why shouldn't I?"* If your dog's a confirmed bolter and you give him the opportunity to bolt—what's to stop him?

- *"Make it worth my while."* A bolting dog ignores your instructions to stay put. That's because the reward of being out and loose is greater than what you're offering. You need to tip the balance in your favor.

HOW TO SAY IT

- *Leash your dog.* Keep a leash hanging from the doorknob on all doors that lead to unfenced areas. Before you open the door, put your dog on-leash. Don't give her the chance to get out!

- *Teach "Wait."* Less formal than "Stay," the "Wait" cue tells your dog to stay put and not follow you until you ask him to. If you have a door that opens to a safe area like a fenced backyard, take your dog to that door, off-leash. Wait for him to sit (this way you'll be teaching him to sit at doorways to the outside). Tell him to wait, then reach for the doorknob. If he doesn't move, click and treat. If he does, just put him back in a sit without admonishing him. (After all, he doesn't know what "Wait" means!) Gradually increase the steps you can take (jiggling the doorknob, opening the door, going out the door), clicking and treating as he succeeds at each step, until you can open the door and walk through it while he holds his sit. Then invite him outside for a fun play session! Keep your dog on-leash when trying this at doors that lead to unfenced areas.

- *Practice, practice, practice.* Ask your dog to wait every time she goes out the door. Use lots of treats. If she learns to sit before doors are opened, she's less likely to bolt through the open door. You can also practice your waits at interior doorways or anywhere in the house.

- *Train a good recall.* If your dog will come reliably when called, you'll be able to get him back in the house if he does bolt. (See the chapter on not coming when called.) This is not a substitute for limiting his opportunity to get loose!

HOW NOT TO SAY IT

- *Don't reward your dog for bolting.* If you chase after your dog once she's out of the house, you're playing right into her paws. If you keep her leashed before the door is opened, she won't have the chance for that great game of catch-me-if-you-can.

- *Don't punish your dog when he does come back.* There's no better way to discourage your dog from coming to you than punishing him (physically or verbally) when he does.
- *Don't give her the chance to bolt.* Until she learns to reliably stay seated when the door opens, always leash her when you open the door to an unfenced area. Keep a leash on the doorknob to make it easier.

chapter thirty-two

Car Problems

Ben's Australian Shepherd, Biscuit, loves to go on car rides. But when she gets in the car, she gets so excited by what she sees out the window that she barks and runs from one side of the backseat to the other. Ben finds it annoying—and distracting. He knows it could be worse, though. His friend, Marlene, has a dog who throws up every time she rides in the car.

Dogs can be such wonderful travel companions that it's a real shame when they can't be comfortable in the car. With some effort, you can acclimate your dog to the car and promote calmer (and safer) behavior. Dogs who get carsick might be helped with some herbs or a change in where they sit in the car.

WHAT YOUR DOG IS TRYING TO TELL YOU

- *"This is just so exciting!"* Some dogs get all jazzed up by everything going on outside the window.
- *"I know we're going somewhere scary."* If the only place your dog goes in the car is to the vet's office or the groomer, she might have very negative associations with the car and be afraid of car rides.

- *"I feel queasy."* The motion of the car is enough to make some dogs feel off-balance and nauseous.

HOW TO SAY IT

For the Anxious or Motion-Sick Dog

- *Administer ginger, which can help a carsick dog.* You can buy ginger in capsules at the health-food store or try gingersnaps—some dogs will scarf them right up. Give the ginger at least a half-hour before you start on your trip and give a fresh dose every few hours for long trips.

- *Crate or otherwise secure your dog.* Wearing a safety harness or being crated might make the anxious dog feel more secure. It will also keep him safer. If looking out the car window is making your dog feel motion sick, you might even try covering the crate like a birdcage.

- *Take the time to get your dog more comfortable in the car—when it's not moving.* Depending on her level of anxiety, feed her treats and do happy things near the car, then next to the car with the car door open, then in the car with the engine turned off, etc., all along clicking and treating for calm behavior, until her negative associations with the car are replaced with positive ones. Then take her on short rides to fun places. Do each step as gradually as necessary, watching for signs of stress.

- *Try a T-shirt.* Putting a T-shirt on your dog might help him feel more secure in the car. This is a principle of Tellington TTouch. (Just ignore the glances of people driving near you!)

- *Use a flower essence.* Rescue Remedy might help your dog's anxiety. Put it in your dog's water several hours before you start the trip and keep giving it to him throughout the trip. You can add it to water, put a few drops right on your dog's tongue, or massage it onto his ears. If you want to be able to dose your dog with it while you drive, put a few drops in an atomizer and mist the car periodically.

- *Try some calming herbs.* If anxiety, rather than motion sickness, is at the root of your dog's problem, herbs like valerian or skull cap might help. You can also buy an herbal combination designed for pets, like Pet Calm.

- *Do some Ear TTouches.* Have a passenger in the car do some Ear TTouches on your dog or do it yourself while someone else drives. Gently stroke her ears, from base to tip, to help ease her anxiety. These touches can also help calm wild dogs in the car.

- *Talk with your vet.* If the problem is debilitating, your vet might be able to prescribe a tranquilizer for long trips.

- *See if your car is the problem.* Try taking your anxious dog for a ride in a friend's car. If she's calm in the other car, perhaps there's something about your car (a sound or vibration, for example) that is causing her stress.

For the Dog Who's Wild in the Car

- *Secure your dog in the car.* A seat belt harness hooked to the seat belt or a crate will prevent your dog from running all over the backseat. It has the side benefit of keeping your dog safer in the event of an accident, too, and keeping your dog in one place can help prevent an accident!

- *Close the windows and turn on the air conditioner.* The breeze might be adding to your dog's craziness. Close up the car and see if that helps calm him down.

- *Reward calm behavior.* Enlist the help of a friend and have one of you drive while the other clicks and treats for quiet or calm behavior in the car. Use a high rate of reinforcement at first.

- *Try a flower essence.* Rescue Remedy might help calm your dog down, as might Bach's Vervain or Anaflora's Tranquility. Put it in your dog's water before you start the trip and add it every time you stop for a rest. You can even rub it in your dog's ears while you're riding.

HOW NOT TO SAY IT

- *Don't feed your dog before traveling.* If your dog gets sick in the car, make sure he travels on an empty stomach.
- *Don't yell at your dog.* If you yell at your excited dog, you'll just add to the excitement. And it certainly doesn't do any good to yell at a sick dog.
- *Don't let it get you upset.* A wild dog in the car can be upsetting and distracting. Take some Rescue Remedy yourself and keep a cool head in the face of your dog's histrionics. It might help your dog calm down.

chapter thirty-three

Chasing Cats

When Patricia adopted her adult Afghan Hound, Sumi, she already had a cat in her family. When Sumi first laid eyes on the cat, Max, she lunged at him in excitement. Max took off running, and a chase ensued. The chase stopped when Max jumped to the top of the microwave. Sumi thought it was great fun; Max was less enthusiastic. Patricia was very upset.

Dogs can certainly learn to get along with cats (and vice versa). Some dogs are more prone to chasing cats than others, and some cats are more prone to running. If your dog is a cat chaser, you'll need to manage the situation, work on desensitization, and reward your dog (and cat) for not chasing (or running).

WHAT YOUR DOG IS TRYING TO TELL YOU

- *"Looks like prey to me!"* Dogs are born with the instinct to run after prey. When most dogs see a running cat, a hard-wired instinct to chase kicks in.
- *"This is fun."* Chasing small animals is highly rewarding to dogs. Until they're taught otherwise, most dogs don't see a distinction between chasing a chipmunk and chasing the family cat.

- *"Why shouldn't I?"* If the cat and dog are allowed to share space and the cat runs every time the dog moves toward her, what's to stop the dog from giving chase?

HOW TO SAY IT

- *Desensitize your dog to the cat.* Keep your dog on-leash, perhaps tethered to your waist or even tethered to a piece of heavy furniture, and let the cat come as near as she'd like. Reward your dog for calm behavior. If your dog can't stay calm that close to the cat, enlist a helper who can keep the cat farther away. Reward your dog and gradually bring the two closer together. Keep the sessions short at first. Don't push it, and be sure to end on a high note.

- *Desensitize your cat to the dog.* Let your cat get more comfortable around the dog by crating your dog and letting your cat into the room with the dog. Give your cat treats for calm behavior around the dog. Slip some treats through the crate door to your dog, too, as long as he's being quiet.

- *Use TTouch.* Do gentle touches on each animal separately. Then, with a helper, work on both animals in the same room at the same time. This should help calm them and make them more comfortable with one another.

- *Give the cat some control.* Use baby gates to stop your dog from chasing your cat into another room. One advantage of the gates is that cats can go over (or under) them easily, while the dog stays confined. This allows the cat to approach the dog. If the dog tries to give chase, the gate stops him.

- *Provide high places for your cat.* Kitty might want to jump out of the dog's reach. Make sure there's a safe place for him to go.

- *Reward the dog for paying attention to you.* Practice rewarding your dog for looking at you (see the exercises in the chapter on inattention), then reward him like crazy when he looks at you in the presence of the cat. This teaches the dog that good things happen when he ignores the cat.

- *Be sure to spend quality time with each animal separately.* Don't banish one of the animals because the two aren't yet peacefully coexisting. Be sure that neither animal suffers from neglect while you work through the transition.

HOW NOT TO SAY IT

- *Don't scream and holler at your dog.* It's easy to get hysterical if you're afraid your dog is going to hurt your cat. But by yelling you're just adding to the problem. Stay calm and trust that the cat will be able to get out of the way.

- *Don't grab the cat.* If your cat's frightened, she's sure to scratch you. Don't try to scoop her up and hold her out of the dog's reach. Let the cat handle it.

- *Don't give your dog the opportunity to chase when you're not home.* Keep the two animals separated when you're away from home so your dog isn't rewarded (or your cat terrorized) by a good chase. Until you can trust them completely, bring the animals together only when you can supervise and reward calm behavior. Some people feel they can never completely trust their dog and cat alone together.

- *Don't punish your dog for cat chasing.* It's so rewarding to your dog to chase prey that your punishment would have to be very harsh and very well timed to deter him. Instead, motivate him by offering an even greater reward for not chasing the cat.

- *Don't rush it.* It might take a number of days or even weeks of training before your dog can be trusted not to chase and your cat not to run. Be patient.

- *Don't mistake play for problem behavior.* It's possible your cat will invite a game of chase, which is okay. You want to avoid traumatizing your cat, but if your cat enjoys it and your dog is not out to harm the cat, let them play.

chapter thirty-four

Counter Surfing

Whenever Lance leaves food on the counter, he can count on his Greyhound, Troy, to jump up and eat it. Troy has scored some tasty treats off the counter over the years—including a whole chicken carcass!

Dogs are natural scavengers, and they see food left within reach on the counter as an invitation to help themselves. It's hard to discourage this natural behavior, so the best course of action is management. If your dog eats stuff on the counter, don't leave anything on the counter.

WHAT YOUR DOG IS TRYING TO TELL YOU

- *"Thanks!!"* Dogs must view food on the counter as a gift from heaven. Smaller dogs might have to work harder to get it, but they'll gratefully help themselves if they can.
- *"What did you expect?"* It's perfectly natural for a dog to help himself to food if it's left out.

HOW TO SAY IT

- *Keep the counters clear.* If your dog has unsupervised access to the kitchen and an inclination to counter surf, don't leave anything on the counters you don't want him to get. It's as simple as that. The microwave is a great place to store goodies you don't want your dog to get. Your counters will be less cluttered, a nice side benefit to properly dog-proofing your kitchen.

- *Eliminate access.* If you must leave something on the counter (to cool a pie, for instance) close off the kitchen so your dog can't get in.

- *Reward your dog for good behavior.* When your dog lies down in the kitchen, even though you're carving a roast on the counter, reward her restraint.

HOW NOT TO SAY IT

- *Don't punish the dog for your mistake.* If you wake up to find something missing from the counter, you have only yourself to blame. Don't yell at your dog after the fact—he won't know what you're punishing him for.

- *Don't provide access to the counter.* If you have a little dog who couldn't get on the counter unassisted, don't assist her. Take away any stools or chairs or covered trash cans near the counter.

- *Don't use aversives.* Traditional trainers will recommend ways to booby trap your counter to keep your dog off—mousetraps, pyramids of cans to tumble on his head, even mats that provide a shock when touched by paws. Why give your dog a nasty surprise when you can manage the situation by not leaving anything on the counter to tempt him?

chapter thirty-five

Destructive Chewing

When Barb and Larry leave their Norwegian Elkhound, Shadow, home alone, they frequently come home to find the remains of some of their favorite possessions. Nothing is sacred: paperwork, watch bands, shoes, furniture legs, even books . . . if it feels good in Shadow's mouth, it gets chewed up.

Dogs like to chew. They need to chew, in fact. What your dog chews is, to a certain extent, up to you. If you give your dog something really great to chew and put away the stuff you don't want him to chew, you'll find your destructive chewing problem will be greatly diminished.

WHAT YOUR DOG IS TRYING TO TELL YOU

- *"A dog's gotta do what a dog's gotta do."* Chewing is fun and rewarding for many dogs. If you don't give your chewer something to chew on, he'll find something himself.
- *"I'm bored."* Dogs left home alone will find things to do when they're not sleeping. For many dogs, that activity is chewing.

- *"You're not giving me enough exercise."* Your dog can't tear up your house if he's sleeping. Make sure your dog gets plenty of exercise, and he'll chew less.

HOW TO SAY IT

- *Develop a chew-toy habit.* Get your dog interested in chewing on the things you'd like him to chew on, like stuffed Kongs or raw or sterilized bones or other safe chew-toys. Make the toys irresistible to him by stuffing them with food and treats. Be sure to supply plenty of these toys stuffed with goodies. Hide them around the house to keep things interesting—they'll help stimulate him mentally. Praise him every time you see him chewing one of his chew-toys.

- *Confine your dog.* If your dog is a confirmed furniture chewer, it's easier to confine the dog than to replace the furniture. A kitchen or a bathroom, which usually has minimal furniture, should be a safe place to confine your dog. Be sure to supply ample chew-toys to keep her occupied.

- *Exercise, exercise, exercise.* As with many other problems, destructive chewing can be helped by increasing your dog's daily exercise. Take him on long walks, get him to the park, take him on jogs, or whatever it takes to supply sufficient exercise so he sleeps much of the time you're not home. If he's asleep, he can't chew up your stuff. This has the side benefit of getting you out there exercising, giving you and your dog more quality time together, and getting both of you in shape.

- *Be patient.* Destructive chewing is a passing phase for many dogs, particularly young adults. Manage the problem by supplying lots of sanctioned chew-toys and putting away things you don't want her to chew. Before long, she might be trustworthy again.

HOW NOT TO SAY IT

- *Do not leave things out for your dog to chew.* If you don't want your expensive loafers chewed up, put them away.

- *Don't abuse the crate.* If you have to confine your dog all day to keep him from tearing up your furniture, don't make him stay in the crate for hours on end. Either use a room for a long-term confinement area, or come home periodically to let your dog out of the crate and have a little fun.

- *Don't ban your dog from the house.* If your dog is chewing up things inside the house, don't banish her to the yard. She can certainly chew things in the yard as well! Your dog deserves the comforts of being inside with the family. Sending her outside will only create different problems.
- *Don't punish your dog when you get home.* Your dog won't know why you're yelling at him; he'll just learn to become anxious about your homecoming.

chapter thirty-six

Digging

Whenever Jill goes out into her once-pristine yard, she wants to cry. The yard is riddled with holes that her dog, Ruger, insists on digging. He's a regular four-legged backhoe. In addition to the aesthetic affront, Jill once suffered a nasty twisted ankle from stepping in a hole she hadn't noticed.

Many dogs enjoy digging. Some do it out of some sort of hard-wired need. Others do it just to amuse themselves. It's hard to stop a dog from digging when you're not around, but you can manage the problem by not giving your dog the opportunity, or adopt an "if you can't beat 'em, join 'em" philosophy and give your dog his own special, safe place to dig.

WHAT YOUR DOG IS TRYING TO TELL YOU

- *"I gotta dig."* Some dogs, like Terriers and some scent hounds, are hard-wired to dig. They were bred to hunt vermin that burrow underground, so digging is part of their genetic makeup.
- *"I'm bored!"* Some dogs dig out of sheer boredom. Faced with hours alone in the yard, they'll amuse themselves by digging a hole. (Or holes.) They think it's fun.

- *"I'm hot."* Dogs will dig a spot in which to lie on a hot day. The recently unearthed soil provides a cool spot to lie in.
- *"Let me out of here!"* Some dogs will start a hole near a fence, hoping to dig themselves out of the yard.
- *"There's something down there."* Dogs will dig to bury things or to dig up already-buried items like bones, cat (or other animal) feces, tasty roots, and any other half-interesting thing they might find buried in their yard.

HOW TO SAY IT

- *Supervise your dog when she's outside.* If you're out there with her and you catch her digging, call her away and redirect her attention to a sanctioned activity, like playing with you or chewing on a chew-toy.
- *Give your dog plenty of exercise.* If he's tired from walking, running, playing, or training with you, he'll be too tired to dig in your yard.
- *Give her a place of her own to dig.* If your dog is a confirmed digger, you can give her a digging box—like a child's sandbox—to dig in. Construct and fill the box (see the following sidebar), then take your dog to the box and encourage her to step into it. When she does, reward her like crazy. This is a perfect opportunity for clicker training. You can reward your dog further by placing some fun items, like squeaky toys and chew-toys, in the dirt for your dog to find when digging. This way, digging in the digging box is more rewarding to your dog than digging in the yard.
- *Cover the area where your dog likes to dig with chicken wire.* This will make digging difficult, even unpleasant, for your dog. But he still needs outlets for his energy, so don't let this be the only way you deal with his digging.

HOW NOT TO SAY IT

- *Don't drag your dog to the hole and scold her.* Dogs don't associate corrections with actions they've taken in the past. All you'll accomplish is to make time together in the yard unpleasant.

Digging

Dogs love to dig. It's part of their ancestry—wild wolves dig dens in which their pups are born. You can satisfy your dog's desire to dig by building a digging box for your dog.

There are several ways to go about it. One of the most simple is to select an area and overturn the soil there to make it inviting for your dog. Or buy a child's plastic wading pool and drill a few holes in the bottom for drainage. Then fill with sand or bedding material for small animals (like hamsters and gerbils). This material is nontoxic and handles moisture well. Or you can dig a hole in your yard of the size you desire and surround it on four sides with two-by-fours or rails, then fill it with a digging material like sand.

However you construct it, encourage your dog to use the digging box by clicking and treating, verbally praising, or otherwise rewarding his using it. Bury some toys and treats in the dirt so he digs up his own rewards. Soon, digging in the box will be far more fun than digging outside it. Attach the cue "Go dig!" or "Backhoe!" when you see him heading toward it, then you'll be able to easily redirect him to the box if you see him tempted to dig elsewhere in the yard. When he's using the digging box consistently, you'll be able to leave him unsupervised in the yard when you want to without fear of his digging up the lawn.

- *Don't fill the hole with water.* This old suggestion simply leaves you with a muddy mess. And the suggestion in a once-popular training book that you hold your dog's head in the water as punishment is too awful to even consider.
- *Don't put things in the holes as a deterrent.* Mothballs or other toxic substances can harm your dog. Your dog can just move to another spot if you fill the hole with his own feces, an unpleasant strategy for both of you. Better to play an active role in redirecting your dog's attention away from digging.

chapter thirty-seven

Escape Artists

Don's Border Terrier, Harry, is a master escape artist. He'll try anything: digging out from under fences, scaling them, even jumping over them. Sometimes Don will look out the front window and see Harry, whom he'd left in the backyard, sitting on the front stoop.

Being an escape artist is an extremely dangerous occupation for a dog. Life outside a securely fenced yard can mean being hit by a car, attacked by another animal, stolen, taken to a shelter . . . it's just not safe. If your dog escapes from your yard, you'll have to take measures to keep him safe. You owe it to your dog.

WHAT YOUR DOG IS TRYING TO TELL YOU

- *"The grass is always greener."* Life outside the fence holds inestimable appeal to some dogs. They get out just because they can.

- *"It's boring here."* It's natural for an active dog who has little to entertain him in his own yard to take matters into his own paws and look for a little excitement on the outside, if he can. Your job is to make sure he can't. (And to keep him from being bored.)

- *"I smell a female in heat."* If your dog is an intact male, he'll do just about anything to get to a female in heat if one is within sniffing distance—which needn't be very close.

HOW TO SAY IT

- *Keep your dog in the house.* Your dog should spend his alone time safe in the house, not out in the yard figuring out ways to escape.
- *Walk the fence.* Carefully inspect your fence to look for any potential means of escape, including holes, loose boards, or faulty latches. Take away anything your dog could use to help her escape like a wood pile or picnic table near the fence. If people go in and out of your yard, put a spring on the gate so it closes and latches automatically. Ideally, you want to find the weakness before your dog does.
- *Plug the holes.* If your fence has a hole in it that your dog manages to squeeze through, fix the hole. Replace that part of the fence or put something very heavy over the hole.
- *Use a kennel run.* If your dog is still managing to escape, or your neighborhood won't allow secure fencing, set up a covered chain-link run on a dig-proof concrete slab for temporary containment of your dog when you can't supervise him.
- *Train, train, train.* If your dog is trained to come when called and you supervise her in the yard, you can call her back from an escape attempt. Or if she does escape, you'll have better chance of getting her back. Training has the side benefit of building your bond and perhaps making her less inclined to escape. But training isn't a substitute for a secure yard. You need both.
- *Neuter your dog.* If your dog is an intact male, his drive to escape will be even greater. A whiff of a female in heat will make him determined to get out. By neutering him, you might rid him of some of his wanderlust.

HOW NOT TO SAY IT

- *Don't leave your dog unsupervised in the yard.* If your dog's prone to escaping, then don't give him the chance. Until your yard is escape-proof, limit his time in the yard to only those times when you can supervise him. Give him his exercise on walks.

- *Don't tie your dog out.* It's not safe to leave a dog tied out unsupervised. Her cable can get wrapped around something or she can be hung up on it. Chaining your dog can make her behave aggressively—other animals or people are within sight, but out of reach, an exercise in frustration for her. Plus, chains and cables break.

- *Don't use an electronic containment system.* Buried electronic fences are popular in some areas. These systems shock the dog through a transmitter in a special collar when he crosses the buried fence line. The fences are hardly escape-proof. A dog can learn that if he runs through the fence line, the pain stops. And that it hurts to get back in. In addition, the fence doesn't prevent loose dogs or other animals from entering your yard, it doesn't eliminate visual barriers to things your dog wants to bark at, and it trains through pain, something that should be avoided.

chapter thirty-eight

Garbage Eating

Whenever Marsha took her mixed breed, Scout, on a walk in the park, the dog would act like a vacuum cleaner, sucking up whatever trash she could find. It got to the point where Marsha had to avoid the park entirely on weekend days, because picnickers were always leaving behind mounds of trash that Scout was more than happy to clean up!

Trash eating can be dangerous for your dog, since dogs can be indiscriminate about eating things, like aluminum foil or cooked bones, that can be dangerous for them. It's one of those behaviors that is so innately rewarding to the dog that it's hard to stop. Sometimes the best you can do is manage the situation by avoiding the trash. But if you work on ensuring that your dog pays attention to you—and that you pay attention to her—you can reduce the amount of trash she consumes.

WHAT YOUR DOG IS TRYING TO TELL YOU

- *"This stuff tastes good!"* Dogs are born scavengers, and most of them just love the taste of garbage and the wonderful crunch of a good chicken bone.

- *"Buzz off!"* If your dog's chowing down on something delicious, he's going to turn a deaf ear to your calling him and even try to ignore you when you're yanking him.
- *"It's mine!"* A dog isn't going to want to just hand over a delicious, ant-covered steak bone. This is where training under less dire circumstance comes in handy.

HOW TO SAY IT

- *Earn your dog's attention.* Teach your dog to pay attention to you when you ask for it, starting under much less distracting circumstances. In the house, frequently call your dog's name, then reward him for looking at you. Do this so often, consistently rewarding the attention, that your dog develops a reflex to being called. (See the chapter on inattention for more attention exercises.)
- *Teach her to drop things.* Again, start in an easier environment. Offer your dog a boring toy, then after she takes it, offer her a tasty treat. Trade her the treat for the toy, then give her back the toy. Once she's dropping the toy reliably, you can attach a cue, like "Drop it" or "Give." If you do this consistently, eventually you'll be able to ask your dog to drop something disgusting—and she'll do it! Be sure to have a great reward ready when this happens.
- *Make your walks interactive.* If your dog puts his nose to the ground in search of something to vacuum up, get his attention with a happy voice and click and treat for his looking up at you. Teaching him loose-leash walking (and, if necessary, head-off-the-ground walking) will help you take walks together where he's rewarded for interacting with you, not sniffing the ground. This interaction provides a nice distraction from the trash. (See the chapter on pulling on-leash for more tips on loose-leash walking.)
- *Know when to say when.* Sometimes trying to get your dog to drop a prized piece of garbage is impossible without a physical struggle. Unless the trash is truly dangerous for her to eat, you might just have to give up, let her eat it, then seek to avoid letting it happen again.

HOW NOT TO SAY IT

- *Avoid the situation.* Don't take your dog to areas where he can get in trouble by eating garbage.
- *Don't let your dog off-leash in garbage-strewn areas.* Without a leash, your dog can turn a piece of trash into a fun game of keep-away. Even if you're in an off-leash park, clip on her leash if you spy trash. Then avoid the trash.
- *Don't ignore your dog.* It's easy to get involved with conversations when you're at the park rather than paying attention to your dog, who can scarf up a lot of trash before you even notice.
- *Don't nag your dog with the leash.* If your dog's walking with his nose to the ground while you try to keep control of him with a tight leash, you'll both just end up in a bad mood. Interact with your dog on your walks, keep his attention with treats and training, and stay away from trash!

chapter thirty-nine

Getting on the Furniture

Dave's Samoyed, Lager, likes to lie on the couch and look out the window. Trouble is, Dave bought a dark-blue couch before he got the white dog, and now it's always covered in white fur. He used to yell at Lager to get off the couch, so the dog doesn't usually go on it when Dave is home. But when Dave comes home from work, he finds the telltale fur on the couch. He's embarrassed to ask anyone to sit there.

Dogs like to be comfortable, just like humans do. When we're not home, it's very difficult to keep them from making themselves comfortable. If it's really important to you to keep your dog off the furniture, management is the key: Don't give your dog access to the furniture.

WHAT YOUR DOG IS TRYING TO TELL YOU

- *"It's comfy here."* Who wouldn't prefer a comfortable couch to a hard floor?
- *"The couch smells good."* You lie on the couch (or bed) and cover it with your familiar scent. When you're not home, your dog can feel close to you by lying with your scent.

- *"Why shouldn't I?"* If you're not home to stop your dog from lying where he's comfortable, what will stop him from climbing on the furniture?

HOW TO SAY IT

- *Provide comfortable alternatives.* Don't ask your dog to choose between a couch and the hard floor. Give him a comfortable dog bed or mat to lie on, and make sure the bed is in the room he likes to hang out in. It's not fair if his only bed is in the bedroom, when he wants to be in the family room with you while you watch TV in the evening. Reward him for lying on his own bed.

- *Teach your dog to get off of furniture on request.* Even if you allow your dog on the furniture, you'll want her to get off the couch when you ask her to. Toss a treat to the floor so she'll get down to get it. If you allow your dog on the furniture, turn this into a game, inviting her on and tossing a treat and telling her "Off." If you want your dog to stay off the furniture, give her something delicious to chew on while lying on a comfortable dog bed. Don't wait for her to get on (then off) the furniture to give her the chewy, though!

- *Don't give him access to the furniture.* If you don't want your dog on the living-room furniture, don't let him in the living room. Use a baby gate or door to close off the room when you're not home. Or make the couch uninviting by placing cardboard boxes or upside-down chairs (or even an overturned coffee table) on it when you can't supervise.

- *Examine your leadership.* If keeping your dog off the furniture when you're home becomes a power struggle, take a step back and examine if you're being a good leader. (See the chapter on leadership issues for more information.) If your dog starts growling at you when you approach her and ask her to get off the furniture, talk with a behaviorist or trainer. This could be a symptom of a serious leadership issue that you'll want to nip in the bud.

- *Cover the furniture.* If your only concern is dog hair, just cover the couch with a sheet or bedspread that you can easily remove when guests come over. Launder the cloth regularly, and dog hair should become a nonissue.

- *Be consistent.* If the family rule is that the dog isn't allowed on certain furniture, don't let him on it sometimes but not others. Make sure the kids aren't sneaking the dog up to snuggle with them. It's okay to designate some furniture as available and other furniture off-limits, though. Most dogs can make that kind of distinction.

HOW NOT TO SAY IT

- *Don't booby-trap your furniture.* Go to the pet store and you'll find devices that will shock or scare your dog when he climbs on the furniture. But if you're following the advice in this book and teaching your dog through rewards and not punishment, why undermine your relationship by using aversives?

- *Don't punish your dog when you get home.* If you see dog hair on the furniture, it won't do you any good to start yelling at your dog for having made himself comfortable when you're not home. He won't know what you're yelling about. Just prevent him from getting to the furniture.

- *Don't make it all or nothing.* It's perfectly okay to allow your dog on one piece of furniture but not another. Dogs can discriminate between the living-room and family-room couches.

chapter forty

Grass Eating

Whenever Nadine lets her Terrier mix, Zelda, out into the backyard, the dog nibbles away at the grass. Nadine worries that this isn't good for her dog and wonders whether it's a signal of some kind of nutritional deficiency. Whenever she tells Zelda to stop, the dog just looks up at her, then continues eating. Even if Nadine takes her right back in the house, she'll start her grazing again the next time she's in the yard. Zelda thinks eating grass is swell, but Nadine finds it frustrating and worrisome.

Some dogs enjoy eating grass. Others don't. But as long as your dog isn't eating grass tainted with chemicals, it's really nothing to worry about.

WHAT YOUR DOG IS TRYING TO TELL YOU

- *"Yum!"* Some dogs think grass is delicious and eating it is fun and rewarding.
- *"I need a little medicine."* Some dogs eat grass (and sometimes other plants) because their stomach is upset. They'll use the grass to cleanse their system by throwing it up or letting it pass through their system.

HOW TO SAY IT

- *Feed your dog some vegetables.* Perhaps you can satisfy your dog's hankering for grass by feeding him some green vegetables. Chop the veggies in the food processor or blender and add them to his food. It's worth a try—and it can only benefit your dog's health.

- *Grow grass for your dog indoors.* You can grow greens for your dog to eat at home, which might well curb his desire to eat grass outside. You'll then know the grass is chemical-free. A favorite species of grass is appropriately named "dog grass." Assigned the Latin name *Agropyron repens*, it is also known as "couch grass" or "quackweed." Sprout the grass in potting soil and harvest it when it is six to eight inches tall. Cut it into tiny pieces before giving it to your dog, or put it through the food processor or blender with other foods. Rye or barley grass works well for dogs, too.

- *Make your own lawn chemical-free.* If you eschew the use of lawn chemicals in favor of organic methods, your dog can safely eat your grass. Doesn't that sound more pleasant than turning each visit to the yard into a power struggle?

HOW NOT TO SAY IT

- *Don't let your dog eat grass that's been sprayed with chemicals.* If you walk your dog in a neighborhood of lush, green lawns that are regularly serviced by lawn companies, keep your dog on the sidewalk. Reward her for walking on a loose leash at your side (see the chapter on pulling on-leash), and save the grass eating for when you're at home.

- *Don't worry about it.* If your dog is eating toxin-free grass, don't let his habit bother you—even if he ends up throwing up the grass. Unless you see other signs of illness, he's just doing what comes naturally.

chapter forty-one

Guarding Food or Toys

Lily adopted her mixed-breed dog, Jack, from a shelter when he was one year old. Jack fit into the family quite well, but Lily is concerned because whenever she (or anyone else) comes near Jack while he's eating or chewing something, Jack will growl.

Guarding resources is a natural survival skill for dogs, but that doesn't make it an acceptable behavior for dogs living in human society. If your dog growls at you or acts uncomfortable when you're near his food bowl or other items he values, you'll want to seek help to modify that potentially dangerous behavior.

WHAT YOUR DOG IS TRYING TO TELL YOU

- *"It's mine."* Food is very important to dogs. Toys or bones can be, too. Your dog doesn't want you to take anything away from him.
- *"I don't trust you."* Not being comfortable with you around his food is a sign that your dog doesn't completely trust you.
- *"I'm the boss."* Your leadership might be in question if your dog thinks he can warn you away from touching his food.

HOW TO SAY IT

Food Guarding

- *Seek professional help.* If you have a serious problem on your hands (for example, if your dog has bitten over food or you think he might), call a trainer or a behaviorist to help you turn the situation around. You don't want to get hurt trying to take care of the problem yourself.
- *Supervise feeding.* If your dog is guarding his food around other dogs in your family, supervise their eating so another dog doesn't try to steal his food. Feed the dogs in separate crates if that's what is necessary for all dogs to be comfortable during feeding time.
- *Avoid high-value food items.* If your dog guards only highly prized items like rawhide or bones, either stop giving them to your dog, or give them to her when she's crated (and, therefore, should feel safe).

Object Guarding

- *Go do something interesting.* If your dog growls over a toy, silently walk away and give attention to another pet or go into the kitchen and cut up some cheese or something. The idea is to get your dog to voluntarily walk away from the toy and come to you. Reward him to high heaven for choosing you over the toy. Distract him with something to munch on, then calmly put away the coveted item.
- *Teach your dog to give you a toy.* Starting with a boring toy that your dog doesn't really value, offer him the toy ("Take it!"), and when he takes it, offer him a great treat you've kept hidden. While he's nibbling on the treat (that you continue to hold in your hand), pick up the dropped toy. Then give him the toy—or an even better one. Practice this several times in a row and, after your dog is readily giving up one object, move on, slowly, to toys that your dog values more highly. If your dog won't give up the toy and your treats are *really* tasty, call a professional for assistance.
- *Put away the best toys.* Keep your dog's favorite toys put away until you choose to give them to him. If they're so prized that they still provoke guarding, put them away until you get the problem under control.

- *Learn to read your dog.* If your dog's growl is accompanied by happy, pre-play body language, the growl might just be an invitation to play.

Guarding Any Resources

- *Train your dog.* Take your dog to a positive training class to help foster communication and trust between the two of you.

- *Work on your leadership.* The guarding might be a symptom of a leadership problem. (See the chapter on leadership issues.)

HOW NOT TO SAY IT

- *Don't leave food or other highly valued items lying around.* If your dog guards her food, make sure you take up her food bowl as soon as she's finished eating.

- *Don't grab the food.* Taking away your dog's food while he's eating just because you can might foster distrust and promote food guarding.

- *Don't punish your dog for guarding.* If your dog is already tense, any kind of verbal or physical punishment will only reinforce her distrust of you and, potentially, result in a bite.

- *Don't put yourself in harm's way.* Unless the object your dog has is dangerous to him, don't turn this into a battle in which you could end up being bitten (and your relationship compromised). Ignore the behavior and work on improving the situation. See a trainer or behaviorist if you feel that the situation might result in a bite.

chapter forty-two

Inattention

Sam's dog, Smokey, pays all sorts of attention to him when they're inside the house. When Sam walks from one room to the next, Smokey's always at his heels. When Sam calls her from the kitchen, Smokey comes tearing in, hoping for a treat.

But when they go out on walks, it's an entirely different story. Smokey is busy sniffing interesting smells, looking for squirrels, and barking at other dogs. She doesn't even turn her head when Sam calls her name. Smokey's giving her dad the big brush-off.

It can be hard for dog owners to compete with the sights, smells, and sounds of the outdoors. But it can be done, if you make yourself very interesting to your dog by rewarding her for looking to you when you call. A simple effort at training your dog to give you eye contact can reap dividends throughout your dog's life.

WHAT YOUR DOG IS TRYING TO TELL YOU

- *"Not now, I'm busy."* Dogs do things that reward them. Checking out squirrels or doing a little detective work with the nose—that's highly rewarding stuff to a dog.

- *"You're not interesting enough."* It's hard to compete with a squirrel or a cat for your dog's interest. But if your dog learns that highly rewarding things come to him when he pays attention to you, he'll start giving you the attention you desire.

HOW TO SAY IT

- *Take your dog to a positive training class.* The process of going through class together will build your bond, making it more likely that your dog will want to pay attention to you, even in high-distraction places.

Exercises in the House

- *Get out your clicker and treats, call your dog to you, and click every time he looks you in the eye.* Do this five or ten times a day for a solid week, and you'll have a dog who looks to you expectantly whenever he hears his name. If your dog doesn't turn to look at you at first, make kissy sounds or in some other way get him to flicker his eyes in your direction, then gradually increase your expectations (and criteria for a reward) until you're getting full eye contact.

- *Play "monkey in the middle."* Enlist a partner to help. With the two of you each armed with a clicker and treats and about six feet apart, call your dog by her name (but don't say "Come" if you haven't yet taught her that cue). When your dog runs to each of you, click and treat. If your dog doesn't come running, click a head turned toward you. If she's clicker-savvy, she should come to you for the treat.

- *Try "hide and seek."* Either have someone hold your dog, or just walk away from her when she's doing something else. Then call her name. Make it sound very exciting to find you. She should seek you out—make it as easy as necessary at the beginning, then increase the difficulty of your hiding places. Each time she finds you, click and treat.

Out on a Walk

- *Now that your dog's learned that you give treats when you call his name and he looks at you, try more distracting environments.* You might have to go back a few steps and reward the slightest recognition of your existence when you're outside. Click if you get even an ear flicker from your dog when you call his name if he's focused on something else. The click should get his attention and have him looking for the treat.

- *Wait for something—anything—to click.* If your dog starts alerting on something and ignores you, stop in your tracks. If she's at the end of the lead, maintain gentle pressure on the leash, call her name, make a kissy sound if necessary, and wait for her to give you some acknowledgment. Then click, and she should come walking toward you for her treat. Just find something to click—even if it's just a flick of the ear after you say something—and you should be home free. Gradually, your dog will learn that giving you attention will result in a bona fide treat, which can be more rewarding than just the possibility of chasing a squirrel.

- *Lure your dog away from the distraction if necessary.* When you're out on a walk and your dog starts sniffing or staring, try putting a treat under his nose to get his attention. Use the treat to lure him into a nice loose-lead walk and click for the walking, then give him the treat.

- *Use the object of her attention as the reward.* Every now and then, let your dog chase that squirrel—after she's given you the attention you've requested. This will be a high-value reward.

HOW NOT TO SAY IT

- *Don't use the clicker as an attention-getting device.* Remember, your dog knows that a click means "What you're doing at the moment you hear the click is good." If you use the clicker just to get your dog's attention, you'll be rewarding his inattention.

- *Don't forget the treats.* When you're in a distracting environment, you're going to need those treats to convince your dog that you're worth listening to. Don't leave home without them!

- *Don't yank on your dog's leash.* If your dog gives you the cold shoulder, don't start yanking her around to get her attention. Try to be patient and use the techniques outlined above.
- *Don't yell at your dog.* Talking louder isn't going to get your dog to listen any better, and you might even startle or scare him. And it's not going to make you any more rewarding than a squirrel!

chapter forty-three

Jumping on People

When Marilyn comes in the door after work—or, worse, when people come to her home to visit—her Golden Retriever, Elliott, always greets her enthusiastically by jumping up on her. Marilyn isn't tall, and Elliott's front paws easily reach her shoulders. He hasn't knocked her down yet, but she figures it's only a matter of time. All her yelling at him to stay down when he jumps on her or on visitors falls on deaf ears. She knows he's just being friendly, but this kind of greeting is sometimes painful!

Jumping on people is a very common habit for dogs. The larger the dog, the more overwhelming, but any jumping dog can be difficult for people who aren't fond of canines. Plus, they can leave behind dirty paw prints or ruin stockings. By understanding why dogs jump on you, and by consistently using some gentle methods, you can make your homecoming a lot easier on you, your guests, and even your dog.

WHAT YOUR DOG IS TRYING TO TELL YOU

- *"Hello!"* Next time you see two dogs greeting one another at the park, take a look at how they do it: They sniff noses. When he jumps up on you in greeting, your dog just wants to get closer to your face to give it a good sniff. He thinks it's a perfectly natural—and polite—thing to do.

- *"I'm glad you're home!"* The highlight of many dogs' day is the moment their owner walks in the door after a day away from home. Some dogs jump up because they can't contain their excitement. Making contact with you is like the physical contact they sometimes make with other dogs.

HOW TO SAY IT

- *Ignore your dog's greeting.* By giving him any attention, including negative attention, you reinforce the jumping up. By ignoring him, you prompt him to try something else to get your attention. If he has his paws on you, simply turn your back on him. If he tries again, rotate away from him. When all four feet are on the floor, you can turn around and greet him.
- *Reward the behavior you want.* If your dog sits down after getting no attention from you for jumping up, give him a treat.
- *Get down to his level.* Your dog wants to sniff your face. If you get down to his level, he can do it without jumping up on you.
- *Have a party.* Ask some dog-friendly people over specifically to work on your dog's jumping behavior. Put some treats in a basket or a bag outside the door, with a note asking people to give the dog a treat when they come in—but only after he sits. Ask each person to come in more than once. The more repetitions, the more practice your dog gets. Hearing the doorbell ring over and over should quell some of your dog's enthusiasm and make him more blasé. This gives you the opportunity to repeatedly reinforce the greeting behavior you want, like sitting.
- *Teach your dog to jump on you on cue.* If you don't mind your dog jumping on you, but would rather he didn't do it to others, pat your stomach and say "Up!" When he does, reward him with a hug or a kiss. If he jumps on you without being invited, turn your back. Eventually, he should do it only when asked.

- *Use a leash.* If you're not able to ask guests to just ignore your dog's behavior, you can use a leash to help her learn how to greet politely. Keep the leash at the door, and snap it on your dog's collar before you open the door. Ask your dog to sit, step on the leash, then open the door. Your dog won't be able to jump up on your guest, although she might try. Ask her to sit again and reward her for sitting. Reserve this method for well-dressed or non-dog-loving guests. With other people, continue to use the methods described above to stop her jumping, and eventually you should have a dog who sits politely, without a leash, when anyone comes in the door.

HOW NOT TO SAY IT

- *Don't yell at him.* It's easy to get frustrated and yell or scold, particularly when your dog is jumping on a visitor. But the yelling doesn't help, and it actually reinforces the behavior since it gives the dog attention. Ignoring is better.
- *Don't use physical means to stop your dog from jumping on you.* Outdated methods such as kneeing your dog in the chest, stepping on his back feet, or holding tight to his front paws aren't effective and don't make sense to the dog, who is behaving very politely, in his view.
- *Don't allow jumping up in some cases but not others.* If you only occasionally reward a behavior, you actually strengthen it. So be consistent in not allowing your dog to jump by ignoring it whenever it occurs and rewarding the behavior you want. Make sure your friends do the same thing when your dog jumps on them, even if they say they don't mind the jumping.
- *If you have a puppy, don't let him jump on you.* Puppies are so darn cute (and small) that people often don't object when they jump up. But your little puppy will one day be an adult dog. If you don't want him jumping on you as an adult, don't let him start now.

chapter forty-four

Keep-Away

Tyrone's Dalmatian, Flash, loves nothing more than to grab something of Tyrone's (like a sock) and run away when Tyrone tries to take it from him. If Tyrone doesn't follow, the feisty Dalmatian runs up to him and dangles the sock in front of him. As soon as Tyrone reaches for it, Flash takes off again. Flash thinks it's fun. Tyrone thinks it is annoying.

Dogs love to be chased. A game of keep-away with Mom or Dad is a source of great fun. But remember, your dog can't enjoy being chased by you if you don't chase him.

WHAT YOUR DOG IS TRYING TO TELL YOU

- *"Catch me if you can!"* Dogs do things that reward them. Getting chased by you is highly rewarding.
- *"I'm in charge of this game!"* It's got to be fun for the dog to be calling the shots, at least some of the time. With keep-away, your dog instigates the game and you end up playing by his rules—unless you refuse to play.

HOW TO SAY IT

- *Make a trade.* If you teach your dog to drop objects when you ask him to, the games of keep-away will be a thing of the past. Remember, dogs do things that reward them, so you'll need to reward your dog for giving up the thing he's grabbed. In potential keep-away situations, give your dog something he values in exchange for the thing he has, which, presumably, you value. This is something you'll want to teach (and practice) before you need it. When your dog has a toy in his mouth, put out your hand for it while at the same time offering him something delicious. When he opens his mouth to take the treat, he'll drop the object. Let him nibble on the treat while you pick up the toy, then give him back the toy after he's through with the treat. He'll certainly learn that giving up an object to you is a bargain. He gets a treat and he gets his toy back. Keep practicing this exercise, adding the cue "Drop." When he has something in his mouth that you can't give back to him, give him the treat and give him a toy afterward. It's a lot easier and less frustrating than a game of keep-away.

- *Ask your dog to leave it.* You can nip the game in the bud by asking your dog to leave it before she ever puts her mouth on the prized object. (See the chapter on teaching "Leave it.")

- *Keep highly valued objects out of your dog's reach.* Don't give him the chance to play keep-away!

HOW NOT TO SAY IT

- *Don't play his game.* Your dog can't enjoy a game of chase if you don't chase him. Unless the object he has is dangerous to him or extremely delicate, try ignoring his attempts to bait you. He should eventually tire of the game and lie down. Then you can offer him a treat in exchange for the object. If you chase him, you reward the behavior and your dog will keep trying to instigate the game.

- *Don't think keep-away always has to be off-limits.* If you enjoy chasing your dog around in play, that's fine. But you should be the one to instigate the game, so you don't find yourself in a situation where your dog's running off with a prized (or dangerous) object hoping you'll chase him.

chapter forty-five

Leash Problems: Lunging

When Peter takes his Standard Poodle, Victor, out for a walk, the normally mild-mannered dog becomes a raving maniac when he spies large, dark dogs. He starts to bark and lunge, even if the dog is on the other side of the street. Interestingly enough, the few times Victor has actually had the opportunity to meet the object of his wrath, he's not acted aggressively at all. But the behavior is enough to make Peter dread taking Victor for walks.

Lunging on leash is disturbing for the human and can be embarrassing, too. It can become such a conditioned response that it can be challenging to change the behavior, but it is possible. Dedicated, consistent training, along with some management, is called for.

WHAT YOUR DOG IS TRYING TO TELL YOU

- *"Stay away from me!"* Although it might look like a lunging dog is out for blood, frequently the behavior is motivated by fear. The dog will lunge and carry on in an attempt to ensure that the object of his fear doesn't approach.

- *"This is what I do when I see [fill in the blank]."* Your dog might not even remember what started the behavior, but he has developed a conditioned response to certain stimuli. It's up to you to change that response.
- *"How dare you come near me!"* A lunging dog might actually be aggressive.

HOW TO SAY IT

- *Countercondition your dog.* If your dog is reacting to something he sees on a regular basis, like big, black dogs, change her response to big, black dogs. Take her to a park or somewhere you can see the stimulus without getting close enough for your dog to be scared by the other dog. Securely tether your dog to a park bench, and when she spies a big, black dog, start tossing delicious treats to her, even if she's barking and lunging. You're teaching your dog that big, black dogs mean treats will come. Once your dog turns to you for a treat when she sees a big, black dog at a distance, you know you're making progress. Gradually move closer to the stimulus over a number of training sessions.
- *Reward good behavior.* If your dog is far enough away that he can see the other dog (or other stimulus) but not react negatively, click and treat his calm behavior.
- *Stay calm.* To the extent possible, don't get upset along with your dog. Yelling at your dog only adds fuel to his fire. Tensing up will make him more tense. As you move to extricate your dog from the situation, try talking happily to him.
- *Visualize success.* It's easy to think the worst when you see something you suspect your dog will react violently to. Instead, visualize you and your dog calmly walking by (or toward or away from; whatever you're going to do) the stimulus. You'll be surprised what an effect this can have on your dog.
- *Talk with a professional.* If your dog is a danger to others or if your dog's lunging is making him so unmanageable that you're not able to give him adequate exercise, see a professional trainer or behaviorist who can help you get a handle on the problem. It'll be worth the time, energy, and money.

- *Manage the behavior.* Until you get your dog under control, try to avoid the things that make him lose his mind. That doesn't mean you should skulk around, trying to avoid other people and dogs. Rather, to the extent you can, plan your walks during low-traffic times. Take your dog to new places—a new park for instance—where habits aren't so ingrained. If your dog only lunges at other dogs or people when he's in very close proximity, don't put him in very close proximity to his stressors until you can work on counterconditioning.

- *Try a head halter.* A head halter will help you maintain control of your dog while you're working to stop the problem behavior.

HOW NOT TO SAY IT

- *Don't tip off your dog.* It's really easy to tense up when you see something you know your dog is going to react to. Try not to, though. Don't let your dog know you're anxious. Instead, take the opportunity to prepare yourself with treats so you can either reward quiet behavior in the presence of the stimulus or work on counterconditioning your dog to the stimulus.

- *Don't worry about what others think.* If you're working on counterconditioning your dog by letting treats flow freely in the presence of something that is making him bark and lunge, ignore the scornful glances you might get from people who think you are rewarding bad behavior. It doesn't matter what they think. What matters is that you are trying to help your dog.

- *Don't stop taking your dog out.* Your dog needs exercise and interaction with the outside world. Don't let problem behavior on a walk prevent you from giving your dog that exercise. Manage the situation by avoiding stressors until you can call in an expert to help you solve the problem. In the meantime, use a muzzle if you're afraid your dog will actually hurt another dog or a person.

chapter forty-six

Leash Problems: Pulling

Every time Walter walks his Huskies, Roy and Blue, it's a struggle. He's tried every type of collar, and even a harness, to keep them from pulling. They pull so much that Walter swears his arms are longer than they were before he got his dogs. For their part, the Huskies treat every walk like it's a sled race. Walter fears his shoulders are going to be pulled out of their sockets or the dogs will lose their walking privileges if he doesn't tackle this problem.

Walks with your dog should be enjoyable for both of you. It's hard to enjoy a walk if you're being dragged down the street. It's actually fairly simple to teach your dog not to pull. It's not a matter of finding the right collar or harness. Rather, you must teach him, with patience and consistency, that he only gets to walk with you if he doesn't pull and that if he walks with a loose leash, he's rewarded.

WHAT YOUR DOG IS TRYING TO TELL YOU

- *"Let's go!"* Dogs learn fairly quickly that if they pull, and you follow, they'll get where they want to go. Thus, they're rewarded for pulling.

- *"Pulling feels good."* Some breeds, like sled-dog breeds, were bred to pull. It feels good to them, and they no doubt think that's what a walk should be. It's up to you to show them that *not* pulling can be rewarding, too.

- *"This is my walk."* If your dog is pulling at the end of the leash, he's not paying any attention to you. Nor does he need to. He's calling the shots on the walk.

HOW TO SAY IT

- *Start out off-leash.* In the house, or in a safely enclosed area outdoors, call your dog and encourage her to walk next to you, without using a leash. When she does, click and treat. This will teach your dog to pay attention to you while walking and that walking next to you is very rewarding. If she doesn't walk with you, or even follow you, liven things up with a squeaky toy, squeaky voice, jumping around—whatever it takes.

- *Make walks fun.* Treats can go a long way toward keeping your dog by your side. Reward your dog for walking near you (and keeping the leash loose) with a click and a treat. You'll be amazed how often he'll choose to be by your side.

- *Be a tree.* If your dog hits the end of the leash, stop moving. Wait patiently until she gives you some slack in the leash, then click. She should trot back to you for the accompanying treat. Repeat this as necessary, but be sure to also click and treat before the leash becomes taut.

- *Use life rewards.* Your treat doesn't have to always be a food treat. If your dog is pulling toward something (like a fire hydrant), stop when he makes the leash tight. When he loosens the leash and looks back at you, click. Then let him sniff the hydrant as his reward.

- *Practice, practice.* Your walks might have to be short at first, but as your dog becomes well mannered on the leash, you'll want to take her more places. Both your lives will be enhanced by your excursions.

- *Just get him out.* If your dog has led a sheltered life and is so stimulated by the outside world that he just can't focus on you while you're out, take him to a park bench (drive him to the park, if necessary), tie his leash to it, and start dropping treats. Get him to focus on treats and on you, rather than on passersby and squirrels. This should take the edge off his excitement about the environment and help him pay more attention to you on walks.

- *Train when she's tired.* If your dog is unruly on-leash, wear her out in the backyard or park with a good game of fetch or tag. Then take her for a walk. After she's been relieved of excess energy, she'll make a better student and you'll have more calm behavior to reward. Another tip: Walk your dog before she's had supper so she's particularly motivated by food.

- *Try some TTouch leading exercises.* These exercises help leash-pullers by employing equipment like leashes and harnesses in a slightly unconventional manner to change the way the dog interacts with you on-leash. (See the appendix for sources of information on TTouch.)

HOW NOT TO SAY IT

- *Don't stop walking your dog because he pulls.* It's tempting to let a pulling dog get all his exercise off-leash in the backyard or in a safe, off-leash area. This might make your life easier. But don't give up. If you teach your dog to walk nicely on-leash, it'll get both of you out in your neighborhood, meeting people and other dogs, and seeing the sights. It's good exercise, a great bonding time, and well worth the effort.

- *Don't jerk your dog around by the leash.* Traditional training methods advocate a choke collar and using leash corrections to get your dog to walk next to you, but that isn't any fun for either of you; it turns walks into a different kind of chore. If you force your dog to walk where you want simply so he won't face the leash correction, he's not a willing participant in the training. This type of training requires a leash, because the possibility that your dog will walk near you if he's off-leash (in a safe area, of course) is pretty small if he associates walking with you with being jerked around.

- *Don't rely on equipment.* Choke chains, pinch collars, no-pull harnesses, and head harnesses all purport to help stop pulling. Chokes, pinches, and no-pull harnesses punish a dog for pulling. Back harnesses are made for pulling—after all, they're what sled dogs wear. Head harnesses inhibit pulling, give the human more control, and can be very useful while your dog is in training. Your dog should walk near you because she wants to—and because you reward her for doing so. You shouldn't have to rely on equipment to do the job for you. For safety's sake, however, leashes and collars are mandatory unless you're in a fenced-in area.

- *Don't run out of treats.* Take plenty of treats along with you on your training walks. You'll be surprised how quickly you go through them, and you don't want to miss the opportunity to reward good behavior. If your dog is easily distracted on walks, make sure those treats are powerfully delicious.

chapter forty-seven

Leash Problems: Reluctance to Walk On-Leash

Julie wants to take her Papillon, Sandy, on walks. But every time she leashes up the little dog and takes her out, Sandy refuses to budge. Julie has tried dragging her, cajoling her, and even picking her up and carrying her part of the way. No matter what Julie does, Sandy just digs in her heels and looks miserable. Julie has all but given up her fantasy of enjoyable walks with her dog.

Although most dogs love to take a walk, some dogs are easily frightened and just won't move. Building your dog's confidence, rewarding even tiny progress, and never, ever punishing her for the behavior can help make the dream of fun walks with your dog a reality.

WHAT YOUR DOG IS TRYING TO TELL YOU

- *"This is scary!!"* For undersocialized dogs, the outside world can be a very scary thing. Some dogs are fine outside if they're off-leash, but the leash takes away their option of fleeing and makes them freeze in place.
- *"You can't make me!"* Some dogs simply can't be cajoled into taking a walk with you if they're too scared to do it on their own. Dragging them by the leash just traumatizes them even more.

- *"Why should I?"* If your dog doesn't want to take a walk, or something frightens her into freezing while on the walk, you're going to have to come up with a pretty good incentive to convince her that taking a step is worth her while.

HOW TO SAY IT

- *Start in the house.* As with teaching a dog not to pull on-leash, you can start encouraging your dog to walk with you without the leash, in a safe environment. In the house, sit on the floor and softly call your dog, encouraging him to walk near you. When he does, click and treat. Then start walking in the house and gently encourage your dog to walk with you. Again, when he takes a step, click and treat. This will teach your dog that walking with you is very rewarding. If he doesn't move, liven things up with a squeaky toy or a happy, squeaky voice (whatever he responds to).

- *Baby steps.* Take your dog out on-leash (on a flat collar) and repeat what you did indoors. Call to her and encourage her to walk with you. If she flatly refuses, calmly wait for her to start moving toward you. Even if she just shifts her weight and leans toward you, click and treat. Gradually increase the number of steps between clicks.

- *Try luring.* Walk toward your unwilling-to-walk dog and wave a tasty and aromatic treat in front of his nose. Then lure a few steps out of him with the treat. While he's walking, click and give him the treat.

- *Build her confidence.* Dogs who are afraid of the world need help building their confidence. (See the chapter on shyness for more information.)

- *Do some TTouches, especially the Ear TTouch, to help your dog have more confidence outside.* You can do it at home or try some touches on your dog when he digs in his heels on a walk.

- *Visualize your dog walking.* Send your dog a picture of her walking happily with you down the street.

- *Talk to him.* If your dog doesn't want to come, walk back to him and gently talk to him about why he should walk with you. Whispered encouragement can go a long way.

HOW NOT TO SAY IT

- *Don't force her.* Don't punish your dog by dragging her along by the leash. If you do, you just make walks scarier.
- *Don't yell at him.* Again, you want to build his confidence, not terrorize him. Yelling only makes things worse.
- *Don't lose your patience.* It's easy to get frustrated by a dog who doesn't want to do what you want—particularly when you're offering an activity that should be fun! If you have a shy dog, take her out for very short walks at the beginning, when you have plenty of time. Once she's enjoying her walks, you'll be able to take faster walks and cover more ground.
- *Don't reward his refusal.* When you click your dog, make sure you do it while he's moving, not after he's stopped or before he's started. You want to reward the desired behavior—movement toward you.

chapter forty-eight

Excessive Licking

Stacey's buff-colored Cocker Spaniel, Barney, licks his paws nonstop. His paws have turned a rust color because of the licking. Stacey doesn't even notice the sound of Barney licking anymore because it's such a constant in her life. Barney simply ignores any attempt by Stacey to get him to stop.

It's not healthy for a dog to lick himself constantly. The licking might be a sign of illness, or it might be a compulsive behavior. Either way, it's not a great way for your dog to spend his time. He could lick himself raw, infection could set in, and then a cycle of ill health could begin.

WHAT YOUR DOG IS TRYING TO TELL YOU

- *"I itch."* Your dog might be licking because he itches. The itching might be because he's allergic to pollens, other things in the environment, or perhaps his food.

- *"I'm hurt."* Dogs lick their wounds, so a sudden bout of licking might be the result of an injury hidden in their fur.

- *"I'm bored."* Your dog might just be licking to keep himself occupied. More exercise, training, and mental stimulation could help.

HOW TO SAY IT

- *Take your dog to the vet.* You need to find out whether your dog is licking because of a wound or an allergy, or whether it's more of a behavioral problem.

- *Give her more exercise.* Your dog can't spend the day licking herself if she's sleeping. If you discover she's licking because of some sort of environmental allergy, be careful about where you exercise her. You'll want to minimize her exposure to allergens.

- *Try a new food.* In consultation with your veterinarian, you might want to switch your dog's food, in case he's itching due to a food allergy. Either switch to a commercial food with different protein sources or try a home-prepared elimination diet, in which you cut back on the ingredients and gradually add more, to try to determine what food is causing the problem. (See the chapter on diet for more information about food.)

- *Talk to a veterinary behaviorist.* If the licking is an obsessive behavior, a behaviorist can help you figure out how to stop it or prescribe medication if necessary.

- *Put a T-shirt on your dog.* A T-shirt can have a calming effect. Put an appropriate-size one on (a baby's shirt can work for a tiny toy dog), with the tag at the throat. Cinch it up at the waist, and tie it in a knot or with a scrunchie to keep it snug. If your dog is licking out of some sort of insecurity, the T-shirt might help. It sure can't hurt.

HOW NOT TO SAY IT

- *Don't let it get too far.* If your dog is licking himself so much that you notice discolored fur, seek help to stop this behavior before your dog starts hurting himself. The licking can cause "hot spots," which can get infected. The hot spots are painful and ugly and can be difficult to heal.

- *Don't put bitter apple on your dog.* Bitter apple is a bad-tasting compound that some trainers recommend you put on items you don't want your dog to chew on. Bitter apple acts as an aversive, which is something positive trainers like to avoid. If you put bitter apple on your dog's paws or whatever body part she's licking, you make your dog averse to her own body. This seems supremely unfair.

- *Don't punish your dog for licking.* Dogs who lick themselves are somehow being rewarded by the behavior. Yelling at them or physically punishing them probably isn't going to outweigh the reward they're giving themselves, and it will almost certainly have a negative effect on your relationship.

chapter forty-nine

Marking

Little Mikey, a Terrier mix, is a big leg lifter. When he and his owner, Marla, go on walks together, Mikey stops to pee on a vertical surface at least five times per block. And he takes the behavior inside the house, too. Despite being fairly reliably housetrained, he'll lift his leg on a piece of furniture if new people or animals come into the house.

Marking territory is natural to dogs. Doing so in the house is unpleasant for the humans, however. Taking care to eliminate any past pet odors, making sure your dog knows where he is supposed to urinate, and neutering your dog can help take care of the problem.

WHAT YOUR DOG IS TRYING TO TELL YOU

- *"This is my territory."* Many dogs lift their legs and pee to define their territory.
- *"My hormones are raging."* Neutered male dogs are less inclined to lift their legs than their intact counterparts.

- *"I'm not thoroughly housetrained."* You might think your dog knows where you want him to pee, but indoor urination might be a housetraining problem, not a territory marking problem.
- *"I can do whatever I want."* If your dog isn't properly supervised or if you have leadership problems with him, he might feel free to lift his leg in the house.
- *"I must tell others I've been here."* The dog who marks repeatedly on his walk is announcing himself to the rest of the canine community.

HOW TO SAY IT

- *Neuter your dog.* If the marker is an intact male, the most important thing you can do to curb the behavior is to neuter him. It will take a few weeks after neutering for it to affect his marking behavior.
- *Clean thoroughly.* If your dog lifts his leg inside the house, be sure to clean the pee with an enzymatic odor eliminator to get rid of, not just mask, the odor. Dogs tend to pee where they (or other dogs) have peed before, so odor elimination is essential.
- *Keep your eye on your dog.* If you catch your dog about to lift his leg in the house, interrupt the act and take him outside to pee.
- *Start from scratch.* Make sure your dog is actually housetrained. For a couple weeks, treat him as if he isn't. Take him out on schedule, keep a vigilant eye on him, and confine him when you're not home. If the indoor marking stops after these efforts, you'll know it was a housetraining problem.
- *Rule out a medical cause.* If your dog starts peeing in the house suddenly, it might be a sign of a urinary tract infection. Talk with your vet about bringing in a urine sample for urinalysis.
- *Look at your leadership.* Is the indoor leg-lifting a symptom of problems with your leadership? Examine your relationship with your dog and make sure you are being the leader he needs. (See the chapter on leadership issues for more information.)

- *Keep your dog's attention.* If your concern is that your dog slows you down on your walks because she wants to pee on every other tree, keep her attention and keep her going at your pace using a system of rewards for walking with you. (See the chapter on pulling on-leash for more information.) Make walking with you more rewarding than marking, or just resign yourself to more leisurely walks.

- *Try a belly band.* If you've tried everything else, or if you're waiting for the effects of neutering to kick in, you can try fastening a piece of cloth around your dog's abdomen to prevent him from peeing indoors (or at least absorb the urine if he does pee—this might be more practical for small dogs). Remove it when you take him outside. It's always better to treat the cause than the symptom, though. A belly band isn't a substitute for getting to the root of the problem and addressing it.

HOW NOT TO SAY IT

- *Don't automatically blame the male.* Leg-lifting isn't a male-only occupation. Feisty females will also lift their legs to mark territory. Marking vertical surfaces is just as important to the female marker as it is to the male one. So if you have a female dog as well as a male, don't automatically assume the inside marker is the male.

- *Don't punish him for leaving a mark.* If you scold your dog after the fact, he won't know what you're punishing him for. If you're harsh with him when you catch him in the act, he'll just be sure not to do it when you're around. If you do catch him in the act, it's best to interrupt the behavior with a sudden sound, then whisk him outside to finish the job.

chapter fifty

Mounting Other Dogs

Ellen's Labrador Retriever, Opie, is a big lug of a dog who loves people and loves to play. To Ellen's dismay, his idea of playing is to mount other dogs. The other dogs usually don't like it much, and Ellen finds it really embarrassing. She tells him no, but he doesn't care.

Humans tend not to like it when dogs hump other dogs. But it's really the dog being humped who should have a say in the matter. If you have a dog who mounts so insistently that he doesn't actually play with any dog (or whose mounting causes fights), you might want to try controlling the situation through some behavior modification.

WHAT YOUR DOG IS TRYING TO TELL YOU

- *"I'm overstimulated."* Some dogs use mounting as an outlet when there's so much going on around them that they don't know what to do with themselves.

- *"I'm the king of the hill."* Some dogs will mount other dogs simply because the other dog will let them.

- *"It's hormones."* An unneutered male might mount as a sexual outlet. Even a neutered male will mount (and try to breed) a female dog in heat.
- *"This is fun."* Mounting is some dogs' idea of a good time. They enjoy it and it's rewarding, so they continue.
- *"I'm nervous."* Dogs who are anxious—for example, those in a day-care situation—might start mounting just to give themselves something to do.
- *"I itch."* In some rare cases, dogs will mount in an attempt to scratch an itch on their underbelly.

HOW TO SAY IT

- *Neuter your dog.* If your intact male is a humper, neutering him might help the problem. Remember that it will take several weeks after neutering for all the testosterone to leave his system, so don't expect instant results.
- *Let it go.* If the dog your dog is mounting isn't bothered by the activity, let it go for a while. If your dog pauses, click and treat, then lead your dog away on-leash.
- *Let the other dog take care of it.* If your dog is annoying another dog by mounting him, the other dog might turn around and snarl or snap. If that gets the mounting dog to stop (as it should), it's the perfect solution. No human intervention is needed.
- *Stop it before it begins.* Closely observe your dog so you can identify what happens before your dog starts mounting. (Does she get wound up in a certain way? Does play last a certain amount of time before the mounting begins?) Then call her to you just before you think she's going to mount. Give her a really delicious treat (you can ask her for a few behaviors first, to give her a longer break from the play), then send her back to play. This way you might be able to interrupt the cycle before she starts mounting.
- *Tell your dog to leave it.* Teach your dog to stop what he's doing when you tell him to "Leave it" (see the chapter on teaching "Leave it"). If the mounting behavior isn't too deeply ingrained, a simple "Leave it" might be

enough to get him to stop. Be sure to reward him handsomely for listening to you.

- *Give your dog something else to do.* Find an activity, like retrieving or running through her bag of tricks, that your dog finds more rewarding than mounting. When she starts the mounting behavior, interrupt the behavior, bring out the special fetch toy, and start a new game.
- *Try a squeaky toy.* If your dog likes squeaky toys, they can be a great distraction. When your dog starts to mount, bring out the special toy and call, "Where's your toy?" then squeak it like crazy. Throw it for your dog and let him play with it.
- *Give your dog a time-out.* If your dog is in a social situation and is annoying everyone with her mounting behavior, remove her from the situation. Take her away and give her the chance to settle down.
- *Make sure your dog gets ample exercise.* Your dog's probably more likely to mount other dogs or even people if he has a lot of pent-up energy. Give him lots of daily exercise so he doesn't have all that energy to get rid of.
- *See the vet.* If your dog insists on mounting and nothing you can do will distract him, take him to the vet to make sure there isn't a medical problem. It's possible that the sheath of the penis has some sort of infection and itches, or perhaps your dog's hormones are out of whack.

HOW NOT TO SAY IT

- *Don't punish your dog for mounting.* You don't want him to build negative associations with other dogs.
- *Don't get embarrassed.* Mounting is embarrassing to humans, not to dogs. Try not to attach your human feelings to the behavior.
- *Don't get mad at the other dog.* If the other dog lets your dog have it for mounting her, don't get upset. It's what dogs are supposed to do. And if your dog listens, it takes care of the situation.

chapter fifty-one

Mounting People

Jessie's Collie mix, Jason, will mount her leg in certain situations. Unfortunately, some of these situations are in public, which embarrasses Jessie to no end. She's at the point where she doesn't want to take Jason anywhere, for fear she'll be humiliated by his behavior. Jessie also worries when Jason tries to mount her little nieces and nephews. He does it when the kids are playing, and it scares them and puts an end to their fun.

Like mounting other dogs, mounting people is natural behavior for dogs. It's actually a little easier to handle than mounting dogs because you have more control over what the mountee does. Making sure your dog is not rewarded for the behavior will go a long way toward solving the problem.

WHAT YOUR DOG IS TRYING TO TELL YOU

- *"I'm overstimulated."* Some dogs will mount because they're so excited they don't know how to contain themselves.
- *"My hormones are raging."* Sometimes mounting is a sexual outlet for unneutered males.

- *"Let me in on the fun."* A dog will mount kids when they're running around and playing together. It's his way of joining the game.

HOW TO SAY IT

- *Turn away.* If your dog starts to mount you or your leg, calmly extricate yourself and take all attention away from your dog. This way, your dog isn't being rewarded for the behavior, which will help put an end to it.

- *Neuter your dog.* You can help those hormones stop raging by neutering your dog. This might help curb the mounting. It will take several weeks after neutering for the effects to kick in, so don't expect instant results.

- *Tell kids to freeze.* If your dog starts to mount children in excitement, tell the kids to stop what they're doing. Calmly go get your dog and lead her away.

- *Teach your dog to "Leave it."* If your dog learns to stop doing what he's doing when you tell him to leave it, you'll be able to call him off when he's humping you or others. (See the chapter on teaching "Leave it.") Give him a great big reward when he stops.

- *Examine your leadership.* Mounting might be a sign of disrespect. Make sure you are being a good leader to your dog and that she respects you as a leader. (See the chapter on leadership issues for more information.)

- *Remove the stimulus.* If your dog gets so excited that he's humping you or others, take him away from the stimulating situation. You can give him a stuffed Kong and ask him to settle down for a few minutes.

HOW NOT TO SAY IT

- *Don't punish your dog for mounting.* Punishment can be damaging to your relationship. And if your dog is mounting as a way to get your attention, you're rewarding the activity by giving him any attention.

- *Don't react out of embarrassment.* What's needed is calm behavior, not overreaction. Although it's understandable that the behavior looks embarrassing in public, there's really nothing to be embarrassed about.

chapter fifty-two

Mouthing

Lena's new puppy, Sparky, is loads of fun. But he's insatiable when it comes to gnawing on family members' hands. His sharp puppy teeth hurt, but no amount of yelling or grabbing can get him to stop. It's become such a problem that Lena's children refuse to play with Sparky anymore.

Puppies explore the world with their mouths, and they love gnawing on stuff. It's up to you to teach them, first, not to bite hard, and second, that your hands—and other body parts—aren't meant to be chewed on.

WHAT YOUR DOG IS TRYING TO TELL YOU

- *"I'm just playing!"* Dogs use their mouths on one another in play, and puppies seem to like playing all the time. Mouthing human family members is a natural behavior, it's just not an appropriate one.
- *"That hurts?"* Puppies who leave the litter at an early age might not have learned from their mom and littermates to inhibit the pressure of their bite. You can step in and teach your puppy bite inhibition yourself.

- *"I need to chew."* Chewing is an important activity for all dogs, particularly puppies. You need to be sure to give your puppy something appropriate to chew on.

HOW TO SAY IT

- *Just say "Ouch."* When your puppy bites your hand, do what comes naturally: Say "Ouch!" Say it only as loudly as you need to make an impact on your dog. You're not trying to scare him or get him more wound up.

- *Give her a time-out.* After you say "Ouch," get up and walk away from your puppy. Close the door behind you or step over the baby gate—just make sure your puppy can't get to you. In doing this, you're taking away what she wants most: you as a playmate. After a minute or two, go back to your puppy, sit on the floor, and start playing with her again. You might have to repeat this over and over.

- *Raise your criteria.* After a few times of being isolated after biting, your puppy might start biting with less pressure. Even if this no longer hurts, you can pretend it does. Wait until one of the nibbles is a little harder than the others, say "Ouch!" and leave him alone. You're teaching him that no amount of biting—no matter how soft the bite—will be tolerated.

- *Give her a chew-toy.* When your puppy needs to chew, give her something sensible to gnaw on, like a stuffed Kong. Freeze it if she's teething and it'll be soothing to her sore gums.

- *Give your dog attention for good behavior.* Don't let mouthing be the only way your puppy gets your attention. Be sure to give him attention when he's sitting quietly (don't wake him up for it, though!) and doing other things you want.

- *Make sure your puppy is well exercised.* If your puppy gets a lot of exercise, she'll be gentler during her downtime with you. Take her on walks and play fetch games with her.

- *Enlist all your family members.* Teach your kids to say "Ouch" and walk away when the puppy mouths them. But make sure they go back to play with the puppy after a minute or two.

- *Do some reading.* Dr. Ian Dunbar, a pioneer in positive puppy training, writes extensively about teaching bite inhibition and stopping mouthing, as well as other important puppy-raising issues. (See the appendix for book and video titles.)

HOW NOT TO SAY IT

- *Don't stop the biting completely at first.* Dr. Dunbar advises not trying to eliminate your puppy's biting before you teach him bite inhibition. If you do, you risk a very bad bite in the future. After your dog grows up, he might be somehow forced to bite you (say, if you slam a door on his tail). If he's never been taught bite inhibition, he won't have any way of knowing to bite softly. After you teach bite inhibition, you can ask your puppy to stop mouthing.

- *Don't grab your dog's muzzle.* By grabbing her muzzle when she bites, you teach your dog to be afraid of your hand near her face. You need your dog to be comfortable with your handling any part of her body.

- *Don't physically punish mouthing.* You'll only escalate the situation, and your puppy will fear you. Instead of physically correcting your puppy, withdraw your attention.

chapter fifty-three

Noise Sensitivity

When Eva drops a pot lid in the kitchen, her Toy Poodle, Thor, bolts out of the room, tail between his legs. The crashing of pans is just one household sound that turns Thor into a quivering mass of dog.

Having a noise-phobic dog can be frustrating—you spend your life walking on eggshells for fear of startling the dog—but it can also be dangerous. A sudden noise could make your dog bolt, pulling the leash from your hand, and run right into the path of an oncoming car. But with some conditioning, therapeutic touch, and supplements, you can turn your sensitive dog into one who doesn't jump out of his skin at a sudden noise.

WHAT YOUR DOG IS TRYING TO TELL YOU

- *"What the heck was that?!"* For many noise-sensitive dogs, it's the surprise of the noise that scares them. You can help your dog learn to take it in stride.
- *"I'm insecure."* Dogs who are easily startled can benefit from some confidence-building exercises.

HOW TO SAY IT

- *Build her confidence.* Get your dog out in the world, take her to training classes and other activities, and increase her exposure to new things. This can help an easily frightened dog gain confidence. The more she's exposed to, the less scary everything will seem.

- *Countercondition him to like the sound.* If there's a sound in your life that occurs regularly, condition your dog to believe that the sound makes good, not scary, things happen. When the sound occurs, give your dog a bunch of treats. Don't worry that he's being rewarded for acting frightened—you're using classical conditioning to change his association with the sound. Do this consistently, and before long, your dog will be looking to you for a treat when he hears the sound rather than making a hasty retreat.

- *Try some TTouch.* TTouch can help improve your dog's response to stimuli. You don't have to do it while she's afraid (although it's okay to do so). Even practicing the small circles and other exercises during calm times can change neural pathways and adjust her response to the scary sounds. (See the appendix for resources on TTouch.)

- *Put a T-shirt on your dog.* TTouch practitioners advocate putting a T-shirt on frightened dogs to make them feel more secure. If your dog is small, a child's T-shirt will do. An adult shirt can work on large dogs. Put the tag in front (on your dog's chest) and tie up any loose fabric at the bottom so he doesn't trip on it. Tying up the shirt makes it snugger and, therefore, more calming.

- *Try some melatonin.* The hormone melatonin can help dogs be less sensitive to noise. (See the chapter on thunder phobia for more information about melatonin.)

- *Cut your dog some slack.* If your dog is afraid of a sound you can avoid, do her a favor and avoid it. For example, if your dog is afraid of honking car horns and you have the choice to take her for walks on quiet streets or busy streets, take her on the quiet walk. Why put her through it?

- *Desensitize your dog to sound.* Get an audio CD from dog trainer and author Terry Ryan, which can help you desensitize your dog to scary sounds. Individual CDs contain forty to fifty minutes of a specific type of sound (car sounds, kids, thunderstorms, etc.), as well as an instructional booklet. (See the appendix for ordering information.)

HOW NOT TO SAY IT

- *Don't reinforce the fear.* If your dog is afraid of a sound, don't soothe him. Instead, show him that the object that made the sound is nothing to be afraid of. If you dropped a book, for example, touch it cheerfully. Then happily take off with your dog in search of a treat.
- *Don't punish the fearful behavior.* Yelling at your dog will only make her more afraid and make her association with the noise even more negative.
- *Don't isolate your dog.* Keeping your dog inside to avoid scary sounds won't help solve your dog's problem. There's no need to take him to a noisy racetrack, but getting him out will build his confidence.

chapter fifty-four

Not Coming When Called

Ann was playing fetch in the yard with her Rhodesian Ridgeback, Rex, and accidentally threw the ball over the chain-link fence. In his enthusiasm, Rex jumped over the fence and started running loose in the neighbor's unfenced yard. Ann grabbed a leash and raced out of her yard, calling "Rex, come!"

But the young pooch was enjoying his newfound freedom and continued running around. As Ann approached him, leash in hand, he'd spring out of reach, creating a fun (fun for him, anyway) game of keep-away.

As frustrating as this scenario is, it's also dangerous. Rex could have chased a squirrel into the distance or darted into the street in front of an oncoming car.

WHAT YOUR DOG IS TRYING TO TELL YOU

- *"You're not enticing enough."* You can't blame Rex for enjoying himself. Running around off-leash is a lot more fun than getting leashed up and going home. It's up to you to make coming to you more enticing than being off-leash.

- *"Chase me!"* A good game of keep-away is a lot of fun for a dog. Chasing and being chased are common ways that dogs play with one another.

- *"There's nothing you can do about it."* Your dog knows that if you can't reach him, you can't do anything to him. If you use physical corrections with your dog and have a history of blowing your cool, he knows it's in his best interest to stay out of your reach.

- *"I can't hear you!"* Certain dogs—particularly sight hounds like Greyhounds and Afghans who were originally bred to track prey with their eyes—become seemingly deaf when their eyes latch onto prey. Scent hounds, like Beagles and Bloodhounds, who track their prey with their nose, have the same selective deafness when they're on a scent. Owners of hounds, or similarly motivated dogs, should take extra precautions that their dogs not get loose and should work extra hard on training a reliable recall (coming when called).

HOW TO SAY IT

- *Call your dog back in a happy, nonthreatening way.* A high-pitched, happy voice will more likely get results than a thunderous, threatening one.

- *Crouch down and hold your arms out wide after you call your dog.* This is a welcoming posture and might result in a big hug!

- *If your dog isn't in immediate danger of being hit by a car, try walking or jogging away from him.* He might worry about being left behind and come running, or he might just think you've turned the tables on the game of chase and be happy to become the chaser, rather than the chasee.

- *When your dog does finally come, praise her to high heaven.* No matter how frustrated you might be that she ran off in the first place or didn't come when you first called, make her feel like coming to you was the best thing she could possibly have done. By all means, communicate your pleasure with extra tasty morsels of food.

- *After rewarding him, calmly clip on his leash, stroke him, then walk away together.* You're letting him know that not coming when called will limit his freedom. As you work on his recall training and he becomes more reliable, allow him more freedom. If he comes the first time you call, reward him, then let him play off-leash some more.

- *Turn it into a game.* In the house, play hide-and-seek with your dog. While she's in another room, go hide somewhere, then call her. Give her as much help as she needs to find you. When she does uncover your location, squeal with delight and give her a treat. The exercises in the chapter on inattention will also help you train a stronger recall.

- *Visualize success.* Dogs are very in-tune with their people. Picture in your mind the glorious sight of your dog running right to you. If your dog is particularly connected to you and you envision him not coming, you might be sending him conflicting messages.

- *Watch for calming signals.* If your dog is moving very slowly when she comes to you, she might be sending you a calming signal. Are you doing something to make her think you're angry? Examine your tone of voice and your body posture. You want to make sure both are happy and welcoming so your dog comes running back to you.

- *Go to training classes.* A basic manners class from a positive trainer will teach you various strategies for teaching a great recall. And the class will strengthen your relationship with your dog and open up new lines of communication—all of which might well strengthen your dog's desire to come when called.

HOW NOT TO SAY IT

- *Don't keep calling him.* If you holler "Rex, come!" five times, he'll learn that there is no need to come the first time you call.

- *Don't run toward her.* If your dog enjoys playing keep-away (like most dogs do), running toward her will simply become a game of catch-me-if-you-can—and an exercise in frustration for you.

- *Don't let "Come" have nasty repercussions.* If you're going to give him a dreaded bath, go to him, give him a treat, take his collar, and lead him to the tub. Don't call him to come, then drag him into the bathroom.

- *Never, ever punish your dog for coming.* You might be angry that it took twenty minutes for her to come, but scolding her for not coming—rather

Dog Talk

Teaching Your Dog to Come When Called

Being allowed freedom off-leash—in a safe area—is a wonderful thing for a dog. Dogs need to be able to run unfettered by a leash, and if they can have an off-leash social life in a safe location, their lives will be fuller. But going off-leash is a privilege that should be earned. Make a concerted effort to train your dog to come when called by always rewarding him for coming.

Start out with him on a short lead and gradually add distance and distractions, always rewarding him for coming, until he comes reliably. Use a really delicious treat that you reserve for coming when called. And don't forget to practice, off-leash, in the house and in a fenced yard. When your dog's earned his off-leash freedom, strengthen the recall by calling him to you, giving him a treat, then sending him back to play.

If your dog has a history of not coming when called, change the word you use as a cue. The new word will become associated with a consistent reward for coming.

You want to make yourself the most enticing thing in his life. If your dog is faced with the choice between coming when called or doing something else rewarding, like eating trash, make coming to you the choice he makes.

than rewarding her for eventually coming—will only make her more hesitant to come the next time you call.

- *Don't stand erect with your hands on your hips when you call him.* You want to keep your posture as nonthreatening as possible.
- *Don't use a thunderous, stern voice when you call.* Give your dog every reason to believe that when she comes to you, you'll be very happy.

chapter fifty-five

Scratching the Door

When Helen's Great Pyrenees, Bear, wanted to go outside, he would scratch frantically at the door to get her attention. To her dismay, his nails started marring the door.

Dogs will scratch at doors to ask to go out or come in, and some dogs will also jump at and scratch the door in protest when their humans leave the house. This kind of scratching can be a real problem for renters.

WHAT YOUR DOG IS TRYING TO TELL YOU

- *"Let me out! Let me in!"* You've no doubt reinforced your dog for this behavior by opening the door when he scratches.
- *"Don't go!!"* Some dogs will scratch when the door closes behind you.

HOW TO SAY IT

- *Put in a doorbell.* If your dog is scratching to be let out, hang a bell on the doorknob (a strip of jingle bells works well) and use a clicker to teach your dog to ring them to let you know he wants to go out.

- *Supervise her in the yard.* If your dog is scratching up the outside of your door to ask to come in, don't leave it to chance. Either go out with your dog, keep an eye on her from the window, or call your dog in after a short period of time.

- *Install a dog door.* If your yard is securely fenced, a dog door can provide your dog access to the great outdoors, without scratching the door.

- *Remove access.* If the problem is your dog scratching at the door behind you when you leave, don't give him access to the door. Contain him in a room away from the door. (See the chapter on separation anxiety for more information on strategies to handle this problem.)

- *Protect the door.* Mount some Plexiglas or foam core to the door so your dog can't damage the door with the scratching. This, of course, doesn't teach your dog not to scratch, but it might be a stopgap measure to preserve the door while you work on the problem.

HOW NOT TO SAY IT

- *Don't open the door while your dog is scratching to get in or out.* Wait until your dog has stopped scratching before you open the door, otherwise you're reinforcing the behavior.

chapter fifty-six

Separation Anxiety

Lydia and her dog, Rudy, are very close. They share a lot of quality time and enjoy a lot of activities together. The only problem comes when Lydia has to leave Rudy home alone. The poor guy just can't handle it. If he's loose, he destroys things. When she crates him, he howls and drools. The neighbors in her apartment building are starting to complain.

Separation anxiety is a stressful problem for both dog and owner. If you can teach your dog to be less reliant on you, he'll be happier when you're not around. Severe cases of separation anxiety might call for a behavior modification program in conjunction with medication. Although it might take some work, solving the problem will make life better for your dog and will allow you to leave the house without guilt!

WHAT YOUR DOG IS TRYING TO TELL YOU

- *"You're everything to me."* Sometimes our dogs can depend on us too much. You'll need to desensitize him to being alone.
- *"I don't have anything else to think about."* Some dogs can be distracted from their anguish at your leaving with some kind of activity that forces them to use their mind.

- *"We spend so much time together."* If you usually spend all day, every day with your dog, he's going to have a tough time if you leave for an entire day. Try to give him some regular time on his own to minimize the trauma when you do have to leave.

HOW TO SAY IT

- *Keep a routine.* Your dog will feel better if he knows what to expect. If you can keep yourself and your dog on a routine, in terms of your comings and goings, you'll help him understand that you are actually coming home.

- *Desensitize her to being alone.* If your dog shows signs of anxiety while you're gone, slowly desensitize her to your absence. Start by leaving her for just ten minutes, then gradually increase your time away from her. If your solo efforts don't seem to help, work with a trainer or behaviorist about designing a counterconditioning and desensitization program for your dog.

- *Give him outlets for his anxiety.* Chewing things can help calm dogs. Teach your dog to chew on chew-toys, not furniture. Start this by leaving him in an area like a bathroom without anything else to chew on. Leave lots of chew-toys with tasty food inside or chew-toys that are themselves tasty. Soon your dog will develop the chew-toy habit.

- *Make sure she gets enough exercise.* If she's dog-tired, she'll sleep more. Give her a good romp or play session, followed by a meal, at least fifteen minutes before you leave the house. This should help your dog settle down before you leave and sleep while you're not at home.

- *Try daycare.* Many communities have doggie daycare, where dogs can spend the day with canine and human company. Or perhaps you have a neighbor or relative who is home all day who'd like some canine company. While you work on getting him past his problems, one of these options might be a way to manage the situation.

- *If your dog has a canine friend, try bringing him over for the day.* The company might be just the thing your dog needs.

- *Try a pheromone.* D.A.P. (Dog Appeasing Pheromone), marketed under the name Comfort Zone, stimulates the pheromones that come from lactating female dogs. It can be calming to a dog suffering from separation anxiety. It comes in a room diffuser that you can plug into a wall outlet in a room your dog spends plenty of time in. Studies show a 72 percent reduction in destructive behavior after four weeks of use.

- *Get a nanny cam.* Leave a video camera running to see if you can figure out what triggers your dog's negative behavior. Does she start freaking out during the first thirty minutes after you leave? That points to separation anxiety. Or is she okay for several hours? If so, you might just have an understimulated dog on your hands who could be helped with more exercise and stimulating toys. (See the chapter on destructive chewing.)

- *Calming herbs might help take the edge off your dog's anxiety.* One herb combination, called Pet Calm, even comes in a chew-stick form. The dog gets to chew—which can be anxiety-reducing on its own—while taking calming herbs at the same time.

- *Try some flower essences.* Flower remedies, like Bach's Rescue Remedy and Anaflora's Missing You, can help address the emotions leading to separation issues. Put some in your dog's water or directly into his mouth before you leave the house.

- *See a vet about pharmaceuticals.* In recent years, the drug Clomicalm has been marketed to help dogs with separation anxiety. The drug must be prescribed by a veterinarian. Some vets prescribe anti-depressants for dogs with separation anxiety as well. The drug should be given in conjunction with a behavior modification program so the dog can eventually be weaned off of it.

HOW NOT TO SAY IT

- *Don't make a big deal out of coming and going.* You put your dog on an emotional roller coaster when you turn each departure and arrival into a drama. Calmly say good-bye (and hello) to your dog.

Dog Talk

Separation Anxiety

What is true separation anxiety? It's a dog's version of a panic attack. A dog suffering from true separation anxiety cannot control his behavior in your absence. He's the dog who whines when you leave the room, who scratches at the door when you're in the bathroom, who hurts his mouth and claws trying to get out of his crate, or who chews at doors and windowsills when kept in a room. If this is your dog (as opposed to a dog with excess energy who destroys things in your absence), you'll want to seek the help of a behaviorist or talented trainer. Your veterinarian might be able to recommend someone. Your dog can be helped, but it will take time for a desensitization and behavior modification program to work. Your vet or behaviorist might recommend medication for your dog while you work on the program.

- *Don't leave him alone too much.* If you work all day and then play in the evening, your dog's going to suffer for it. Try to minimize your evenings out when your dog has been home alone all day, or start participating in leisure-time activities that can include your dog, too.
- *Don't punish misbehavior.* Downplay any transgressions that happen in your absence. Your dog doesn't know what you're punishing him for, but if he knows you always punish him when you get home, his anxiety will just increase.
- *Don't reward the anxiety.* If your dog whines for your attention when you're home, don't rush to him to reassure him that you're there. You'll just teach him to cry when you're not in his presence.
- *Don't rush to add a new family member.* It's possible that if your dog had company at home, like another dog or cat, he would miss you less. But adding another animal to your family is no small matter. Give the commit-

ment of time and money very careful consideration. And be aware that if you add another dog, you might end up with two dogs who destroy the house in your absence!

- *Don't crate your dog.* If your dog panics in the crate because of separation anxiety, don't increase his anxiety by crating him. Try a room with nothing in it to destroy and see if he can remain calm in there with a stuffed Kong toy or bone.

chapter fifty-seven

Shyness

Ann's Shetland Sheepdog, Angel, is very uncomfortable with strangers. If an unfamiliar person approaches her, she barks and backs away. No amount of sweet talk from the new person will entice her to approach, not even for a treat. Ann's afraid that someday Angel will bite someone if she's backed into a corner, so she avoids the situation by leaving Angel at home and not inviting anyone into her house.

Angel's behavior is based in fear. Perhaps she wasn't properly socialized as a puppy, or maybe it's a trait she was born with. Isolating her isn't the answer. You can help your shy dog overcome her fear of strangers by instituting a program of counterconditioning and desensitization, changing her association with strangers and making her more comfortable with them.

WHAT YOUR DOG IS TRYING TO TELL YOU

- *"People are scary!"* For whatever reason, your shy dog is afraid that unfamiliar people will hurt her. She needs to learn that they can be the bearers of good things!

- *"Noises are scary!"* Some dogs are scared to death of noises that other dogs barely pay any attention to. Desensitization can help.
- *"Ouch!"* Your dog might be acting fearfully because she's in pain or is feeling poorly.

HOW TO SAY IT

- *Rule out physical problems.* Take your dog to the vet and make sure he doesn't have a health problem that's contributing to his shyness. If his vision or hearing is impaired, for example, he might be more fearful. Low thyroid levels, which are not uncommon in dogs, can lead to grumpiness, as can pain.
- *Use a soft voice with your dog.* Speaking harshly when you ask your shy dog for behaviors will probably frighten her.
- *Take your dog on short walks, keeping your voice happy and helping him focus on you with treats.* As he's more comfortable with your neighborhood, expand his horizons and take him to parks, pet-supply stores, or other places where dogs are allowed. It's up to you to protect him from challenges by strangers, though; ask people not to touch him and not to look him in the eye if he's not ready for it. (See the chapter on reluctance to walk on-leash for more tips about walks.)
- *Stay relaxed yourself.* Your dog will pick up on your emotions. If you're worried about how your dog is going to behave when encountering a stranger, you'll nonverbally communicate that worry to him. Do what you need to do to allay your own worry (for example, muzzle your dog—after carefully introducing him to it, using lots of treats—if you're worried he's going to bite), so you can reassure your dog with your calm demeanor.
- *Get your friends to offer tasty treats to your dog.* Instruct them to do so in a nonthreatening manner with no direct eye contact and make sure the treats are really wonderful. Once your dog is taking treats from your friends, start asking friendly-looking strangers in the park to participate. Soon your dog will learn that unfamiliar people mean something good.

- *Watch her body language.* Know the cues your dog gives with her body so you can tell when she's frightened. And know what she looks like when she's relaxed, so you can reward subtle shifts toward relaxation.
- *Look for calming signals.* If your dog starts sniffing the ground or yawning as a friend approaches, it might be too much too soon. Have your friend back off for now and give your dog treats yourself while your friend stays at a distance that's comfortable for your dog.
- *Send your dog some calming signals.* When your dog gets nervous, try some of the calming signals outlined in the introduction of this book. You might find that just yawning at your dog will help him relax!
- *TTouch can be very helpful for fearful dogs.* Hire a TTouch practitioner in your area, attend a seminar, read one of TTouch founder Linda Tellington-Jones's books, or watch one of her videos on TTouch to try it yourself. (See the appendix for contact information and book and video titles.)
- *Go into training.* Training classes will build your bond with your dog, give your dog confidence, and give the two of you a shared vocabulary. Your dog will learn to focus on you, rather than run away in fear, when faced with something scary. Be sure to talk with your instructor in advance about the fact that your dog is shy and make sure you're comfortable with the instructor's methods for dealing with your shy dog. If your instructor uses harsh methods or does anything to your dog that you're not comfortable with, look elsewhere for classes.
- *Try agility.* After your dog has some basic training under her belt and is comfortable in a classroom setting, you might try agility, a sport in which dogs go through an obstacle course. Mastering agility can help build your dog's confidence—it's fun for both you and your dog and it gives her the opportunity to succeed. Remember, if necessary, to protect your dog from approaching strangers by telling people how to behave around your dog.
- *Try a head halter.* The gentle pressure of a head halter, which attaches around a dog's muzzle and behind his ears (think of a horse halter), can be

reassuring for a shy dog. It also gives you more control of your dog than a regular collar does. There are several types of head halters, including the Gentle Leader, Halti, and Snoot Loop.

- *Seek out your peers.* Talk to other owners of shy dogs for mutual support and assistance. On the Internet, look for the shy-k9s group, which was hosted by yahoogroups.com at press time. These groups can provide a wealth of information and, very important, let you know you're not alone.

- *See a behaviorist.* If your dog has bitten or nipped out of fear, talk to a qualified behaviorist about a program to help your dog become less fearful. Your veterinarian might be able to recommend a good behaviorist.

HOW NOT TO SAY IT

- *Don't isolate your dog.* Not taking your shy dog out in the world because he's scared is actually the worst thing you can do for him. Instead, you'll want to get him out and about, while protecting him from scary things and slowly getting him more comfortable with the world.

- *Don't let strangers pet your dog.* Until your dog is comfortable around strangers, don't frighten your dog further by letting strangers touch her. It can be hard to assert yourself to strangers (especially if you're shy yourself), but your dog depends on you to protect her.

- *Don't force your dog to greet people.* If a person wants to greet your dog, don't force it if your dog is uncomfortable. You might put your dog in a position of having to lash out if you drag him to the friendly person.

- *Don't announce your fears to your dog by tightening his leash and keeping it tight when your dog is approached by a stranger.* He'll pick up on your tension, which will make him less comfortable with the stranger.

- *Don't let her off-leash.* Unless you're in a secure area, without other dogs around, you're asking for trouble if you let your shy dog off-leash. Something could spook her and cause her to bolt. A person or dog could scare her and she could bite. Save the off-leash recreation for after she's more comfortable with the world and less likely to run away in fear.

- *Don't reward fear.* When your dog is acting fearful, resist the urge to comfort and coddle him. Instead, stay upbeat and talk enthusiastically to him until he displays more calm behavior, then reward that behavior.

chapter fifty-eight

Stool Eating

Mandy is a lovely dog with a distasteful habit: She'll eat stools. Her own, those from other dogs, cats, or other animals—she doesn't care. Her owner, Maria, finds it disgusting and tries to prevent Mandy from kissing her because she's so grossed out.

Stool eating (technically known as coprophagia) is a natural habit for dogs. Fortunately, not all dogs indulge in it, but if your dog does, you can try a few things to minimize it.

WHAT YOUR DOG IS TRYING TO TELL YOU

- *"Yum!"* Some dogs just like the taste of poop. It's just one of many flavors that appeal to dogs that don't appeal to humans.
- *"I need it."* Stool eating can be a sign of nutritional deficiency in some dogs. Perhaps your dog isn't digesting his food effectively or isn't getting everything he needs from his food. Whatever the deficiency, he might be trying to get nutrients from the stool he's eating.

HOW TO SAY IT

- *Pick up the poop.* If your main problem is your dog eating his own feces in the yard, don't give him a chance. Go out in the yard with him when he defecates and clean it up. This has the added benefit of giving you the opportunity to monitor his stool, which can be an important indicator of his health.

- *Add some enzymes.* Digestive enzymes (one popular product made for dogs and cats is called Prozyme) can help your dog get maximum nutrition from her food by helping her digest it better. If her food is well digested, her stool will be less nutritious, and her need for extra nutrition will be reduced. It might just solve the problem.

- *Upgrade the food.* Try buying a higher-quality brand of dog food, one whose nutrients might be more available to your dog. Or do some research and start preparing food for your dog yourself. By maximizing nutrition, you might minimize your dog's desire to eat stools. (See the chapter on diet for more information.)

- *Make the cat's litter box inaccessible.* It's very hard to discourage your dog from raiding the litter box. Instead, you should use whatever means necessary to keep the litter box out of your dog's reach. If your dog is bigger than your cat, use a long hook and eye to keep the door to the room where the litter box is kept open just enough for the cat to enter (or cut a cat-size hole in the door). If your dog is smaller than your cat, perhaps a baby gate (which the cat can jump over but the dog can't) will do the trick.

- *Leash him.* So your dog likes to eat poop when he's running off-leash in the park? If you can't control that behavior, leash him until you can. Make your walks in the park on-leash until your voice control over him is stronger.

- *Stop worrying about it.* If you offer him more nutritious food and maximize digestibility, you could try to just let it go. Stool eating is disgusting by human standards, but from a dog's point of view, it's really not that big a deal. Especially if your dog eats the stool of vegetarian animals (like deer and cows), the stool should do him no harm. You might not want him licking your face, though.

HOW NOT TO SAY IT

- *Don't yell about it.* As any owner of a confirmed stool eater will tell you, yelling while your dog is eating poop isn't going to stop him. You're better off trying to manage the situation by avoiding areas where poop is available and teaching your dog that great things come from you when you call him. After some positive training, your dog will think you're more attractive than poop!

chapter fifty-nine

Thunder Phobia

Whenever there was a thunderstorm, Lori's Spaniel, Nell, would lose her mind out of fear. She'd start acting agitated long before the storm hit, and whenever there was a clap of thunder she'd turn into a wild dog, scratching at walls, digging at corners, running from room to room. Lori became very attentive to weather forecasts during storm season and tried to stay home during storms to keep her dog safe, but she wished there was more she could do to help calm her dog during storms.

Thunder phobia can be debilitating for many dogs and their owners. It's heartbreaking to see your dog so frightened. But your dog needn't suffer unaided. Depending on the severity of the fear, a number of natural remedies might help, as can behavior modification. If those don't work, pharmaceuticals might help keep your dog's frenzy at bay.

WHAT YOUR DOG IS TRYING TO TELL YOU

- *"This is scary."* Thunderstorms are scary business, plain and simple. They're loud, unpredictable, and uncontrollable. To top it off, there's an undercurrent of electricity.

- *"It's too much!"* Thunderstorms are more than just noise. There's the rumbling of the thunder and the accompanying vibrations, the lightning, the rain, the change in atmospheric pressure . . . it all adds up to sensory overload for your dog.

- *"This is what I'm supposed to do during storms."* A dog who has spent a lifetime being reassured during thunderstorms might come to the conclusion that it's an appropriate, expected response.

HOW TO SAY IT

- *Stay upbeat.* If your dog isn't severely freaked out, try being positive and upbeat in the face of the storm. Throw a ball, play with him, and see if you can get his mind off the storm and his fear.

- *Try some flower essences.* Rescue Remedy or single essences like Mimulus (for fear of known things) or Rock Rose (for terror) might help. Put a few drops of the essences in your dog's water, or right onto her tongue, at the first sign of a thunderstorm. You can even put some in water and mist it over your dog. Don't give up if you don't see progress. Keep administering every half-hour or so and keep it up during at least a few thunderstorms. Frequency, rather than dosage, is the key to success.

- *Administer melatonin.* This hormone, found at health-food stores, is used by humans to help with insomnia and jet lag. It has also been used successfully in dogs for thunder phobia. The standard dosage for humans is 3 milligrams, which is a good starting point for large dogs. Small dogs could get half that, and giant dogs twice as much. Consult your veterinarian for further dosage information. Also, talk with your veterinarian before administering if your dog has autoimmune diseases or any other serious chronic illness.

- *Try l-theanine.* This amino acid can be calming for mildly thunder-sensitive dogs. It's safe and fast-acting. Give one capsule a half-hour before the storm, if possible, or when your dog starts to fret. (See the appendix for a source.)

- *Give your dog some calming herbs.* Herbs like valerian, chamomile, or kava kava can have a calming effect on your dog. Look for calming herbal remedy combinations created for animals, like Calm Pet from NutriBest, or the Animal Apawthecary's Tranquility Blend, or consult a holistic vet for specific recommendations.

- *Put a T-shirt on your dog.* Strange as it might sound, a T-shirt can be very calming to dogs, say practitioners of Tellington TTouch. Put it on so that the back of the shirt (where the tag is) is on the dog's chest. Tie any excess into a knot at the waist or hold it together with a scrunchie or elastic hair band.

- *Create a safe haven for your dog.* Fixing your dog a comfy bed in a closet might help him feel less frantic. Some dogs like to be in a dry bathtub where they're grounded from the electricity in the air.

- *Give D.A.P. a try. The Dog Appeasing Pheromone*, marketed under the name Comfort Zone, stimulates the comforting pheromones that lactating bitches emit to their puppies. Confining your dog to a safe room during a storm and plugging a D.A.P. diffuser into wall might help keep her more calm when the thunder claps.

- *Try TTouch.* Although the hands-on technique of gentle circular massage might not have an immediate impact during a thunderstorm, it might help your dog if you perform it during calm weather when your dog is relaxed—it disrupts neural pathways and creates changes at the cellular level, thereby generating new responses to stimuli. It's easy to do, pleasurable for your dog, and certainly worth a try.

- *Talk to a behaviorist.* A behaviorist can help you put together a desensitization program to help your dog get over his fear of thunder. Such programs can take a concerted effort, but if it rids your dog of this debilitating fear, it can be worth it.

- *Do some reading.* The April 2000 and May 2000 issues of *The Whole Dog Journal* have excellent, comprehensive articles on treating thunder phobia. (See the appendix for information on ordering articles or back issues.)

- *Get a prescription.* Some tranquilizers like Valium and Acepromazine (frequently given in combination) can sedate your dog and keep his panic at bay during a thunderstorm. The medications must be given before the storm begins. They'll leave your dog groggy and affect his coordination, and they don't address the source of the problem. But if natural remedies or desensitization don't work, they can help keep your dog safe during storms. Talk with your vet about pharmacologic (and other) options before administering these or any other drugs for thunder phobia.

HOW NOT TO SAY IT

- *Don't coddle or reassure your dog.* If you try to make your dog feel better by holding or soothing her, you'll reinforce the behavior.
- *Don't give up too soon.* Don't try a remedy once and discard it if you don't see immediate results. Some natural therapies can have a cumulative effect, so give it during several thunderstorms before deciding it doesn't work.
- *Don't try too many potential solutions at once.* You'll want to know which solution is working, so be careful how you combine remedies. Keep close track of what you've tried and what works.

chapter sixty

Trash-Basket Raiding

Tina came home from work one day to find what looked like a paper blizzard in her bathroom. Her dog, Buttons, had amused herself by emptying the contents of the bathroom trash basket and shredding everything. This was a little messy to clean up, but it wasn't as bad as the time Buttons raided the kitchen trash and ate chicken bones and tin foil.

Some dogs are true garbage hounds. Nothing, not even tissues, is safe from their raids. It's very difficult to train your dog to stay away from the trash when you're not around to stop him, so don't let him get to the trash in the first place.

WHAT YOUR DOG IS TRYING TO TELL YOU

- *"This stuff tastes good!"* Trash cans are often full of stuff that tastes great to dogs. Unfortunately, some of that stuff, like cooked chicken bones or chocolate or foil, can be dangerous to your dog. But he doesn't care.
- *"This is fun!"* Some dogs really enjoy shredding paper, particularly tissues. Rooting around in a trash bin can be lots of fun, too.

- *"It smells like you."* Used tissues, in particular, hold an attraction for many dogs, possibly because they smell like the person who used them. Take it as a compliment!
- *"Why shouldn't I?"* Trash-basket raiding is rewarding for your dog. If the basket's just sitting there, what's to stop him from taking advantage of the situation?

HOW TO SAY IT

- *Put away the trash.* This one's a no-brainer. Don't leave the trash out for your dog to get. If this means taking out the kitchen trash every single day, so be it. Put the bathroom trash in the linen closet or inside the shower stall. Do what you have to do. If you have a trash raider, don't tempt him!
- *Try bungee cords.* If for some reason you can't get your trash out of your dog's reach, use a can with a lid and try bungee cords to keep the lid on tight.
- *Give your dog plenty of exercise.* If your dog is tired out by the time you go to work, he'll snooze rather than explore.

HOW NOT TO SAY IT

- *Don't leave delectable stuff in the trash.* Take that chicken carcass to the trash bins outside rather than tempting your dog by leaving it in the kitchen trash. Even the most well-behaved dog might find that to be too much temptation!
- *Don't punish the dog for your own error.* If you've left the trash out for your dog to get to, it's your own fault.

chapter sixty-one

Submissive Urination

Whenever Joel comes home, his little Bichon Frisé, Snowball, rushes to greet him at the door. But as soon as he bends down to greet her, she pees. This messy habit is a source of frustration for Joel and, when Joel lets her know about his displeasure, it's no picnic for Snowball, either. In fact, his displeasure makes the problem worse.

Elimination issues like these can really damage a relationship. If Joel recognizes why Snowball is urinating, he can help solve the problem. Dogs who urinate submissively need to have their self-confidence boosted.

WHAT YOUR DOG IS TRYING TO TELL YOU

- *"You're the boss."* By submissively urinating, your dog is trying to appease you. It's a compliment, in a way, even if it is a messy one.
- *"I come in peace."* One way a dog tells another dog that he means no harm is to urinate. When a dog consistently urinates upon greeting you or when you yell at her, she's letting you know that she is not going to challenge you. This can happen even if you've never had any kind of conflict.

HOW TO SAY IT

- *Greet your dog in a quiet, calm voice.* Don't get her worked up with an overly enthusiastic greeting. If she still pees, try ignoring her completely when you walk in the door.
- *Ask your dog to sit before greeting you.* Reward his sitting with calm praise and a little treat.
- *Ignore any submissive urination.* Then leave the house and come back in again. Ask her to sit. If she doesn't urinate on the second (or third or fourth) greeting, reward her with a treat.
- *Crouch down to greet him.* By putting yourself at his level, you'll be less threatening.
- *Build your dog's confidence by exposing her to other people and dogs.* Take her to a training class or park where she can meet other dogs. And invite people over to your home. Ask all your visitors to greet her calmly, without reprimand for any submissive urination. (See the chapter on shyness for more information on socializing shy dogs.)
- *Try an ear touch.* The Ear TTouch, where the dog's ear is stroked from base to tip, can help with submissive urination.

HOW NOT TO SAY IT

- *Do not yell at your dog for submissively urinating.* This will only strengthen her fear and her need to let you know that she means no harm. She'll pee even more.
- *Don't use any physical punishment with your dog—for any infraction.* By punishing your dog, you'll make him more nervous about you and your intentions.
- *Don't stand over her when you greet her.* This might threaten her.
- *Don't be too enthusiastic with your praise when she doesn't pee.* Your enthusiasm might make her pee.

chapter sixty-two

Yard and Landscape Destruction

Before they adopted their German Wirehaired Pointer, Harley, Amy and Gary had a beautifully landscaped backyard. Amy was an avid gardener, and the yard boasted beds full of unusual flowers and a pristine lawn. But Harley changed everything. Before they knew it, flowers were trampled and the lawn was sprinkled with brown spots and even bare patches.

Dogs can be hard on yards, there's no denying it. But if your dog doesn't spend much unsupervised time in the yard and you plan your garden carefully, you can enjoy both a pretty lawn and a happy pooch.

WHAT YOUR DOG IS TRYING TO TELL YOU

- *"A dog's gotta run."* Your dog's going to run around in your yard, and he will trample what he steps on.
- *"Plants are to pee on."* If your dog has free run of the yard, he will, no doubt, pee on your prize petunias.
- *"I'm bored."* Destructive behavior in the yard, like digging, might be due to sheer boredom.

HOW TO SAY IT

- *See where your dog likes to run in the yard and plant accordingly.* Most dogs like to run along the fence, so don't plant anything there that you don't want destroyed.

- *Leave a running strip.* If your dog likes to run along the fence, plant tall border plants a foot or so away from the fence. Your yard will still look good, but your dog will have plant-free areas in which to run and the bare track will be masked.

- *Try raised beds.* If you section off your planting beds, you provide a visual barrier that will be easier for your dog to respect. When your dog starts to clamber atop the beds, call her off and reward her for playing in sanctioned areas.

- *Fence off the plants.* If you're very concerned about your dog going near your plants, put a fence around the planting beds.

- *Give him a digging box.* If your dog's a big digger, make a place where he's allowed to dig. (See the chapter on digging for more information.)

- *Exercise your dog outside the yard.* Take your dog for walks or to the park for her exercise. That way she can enjoy a nap on the patio while you enjoy your garden in the evening.

- *Create a potty area.* If you're worried about your dog's urine turning the grass yellow, make an area for him to go to the bathroom. Until the habit is ingrained, walk him out to the potty area, on-leash if necessary, and reward him for using it.

HOW NOT TO SAY IT

- *Don't leave your dog unsupervised in the yard.* You have no way of controlling her behavior if she's out there by herself. She's also more likely to be bored and destructive if she's alone in the yard.

- *Don't blame your dog.* Dogs don't have respect for plants. Why should they? Don't expect your dog to care what type of plant he's walking on or peeing on.

- *Don't garden with plants that could be dangerous.* Plants that can be poisonous to dogs if ingested include azaleas, geraniums, daffodils, foxglove, and lily of the valley. (See the appendix for sources of information on dangerous plants.)

Appendix

Resources for Further Information

GENERAL CARE/RELATIONSHIP-BUILDING

Adams, Janine. *25 Stupid Mistakes Dog Owners Make*. Los Angeles: Lowell House, 2000.

Clothier, Suzanne. *Bones Would Rain from the Sky: Deepening Our Relationships with Dogs*. New York: Warner Books, 2002.

McConnell, Patricia B., Ph.D. *The Other End of the Leash: Why We Do What We Do Around Dogs*. New York: Ballantine Books, 2002.

Miller, Cynthia D. *Canine Adventures: Fun Things to Do with Your Dog*. Yuba City, CA: Animalia Publishing, 1999.

The Whole Dog Journal
Subscriber services:
P.O. Box 420235
Palm Coast, FL 32142-0235
1-800-829-9165
www.whole-dog-journal.com
The Whole Dog Journal provides a wealth of cutting-edge information on positive training and holistic health and nutrition issues. It's not available on the newsstand, and it doesn't accept advertising. Individual articles are available for purchase on the website,

and back issues can be ordered from subscriber services. *WDJ* is an excellent resource for anyone interested in progressive training and healthcare for their dog.

TRAINING/BEHAVIOR

Books

Alexander, Melissa. *Click for Joy!* Waltham, MA: Sunshine Books, 2003.

Arden, Andrea. *Dog Friendly Dog Training.* Foster City, CA: Howell Book House/IDG Books Worldwide, 1999.

Book, Mandy, and Cheryl S. Smith. *Quick Clicks: 40 Fast and Fun Behaviors to Train with a Clicker.* Carlsborg, WA: Legacy by Mail, 2001.

Booth, Sheila. *Purely Positive Training: Companion to Competition.* Unionville, NY: Podium Publications, 1998.

Dodman, Nicholas. *Dogs Behaving Badly: An A-to-Z Guide to Understanding and Curing Behavioral Problems.* New York: Bantam Books, 1999.

———. *The Dog Who Loved Too Much: Tales, Treatments and the Psychology of Dogs.* New York: Bantam Books, 1996.

Donaldson, Jean. *The Culture Clash.* Berkeley, CA: James and Kenneth Publishers, 1996.

———. *Dogs Are from Neptune.* Berkeley, CA: James and Kenneth Publishers, 1998.

Dunbar, Ian. *After You Get Your Puppy.* Berkeley, CA: James and Kenneth Publishers, 2001.

———. *Before You Get Your Puppy.* Berkeley, CA: James and Kenneth Publishers, 2001.

———. *Dog Behavior: An Owner's Guide to a Happy, Healthy Pet.* New York: Howell Book House/Macmillan General Reference, 1999.

———. *How to Teach a New Dog Old Tricks.* Berkeley, CA: James and Kenneth Publishers, 1998.

Jones, Deborah. *Clicker Fun: Dog Tricks and Games Using Positive Reinforcement.* Eliot, ME: Howln Moon Press, 1998.

McConnell, Patricia. *The Cautious Canine: How to Help Dogs Conquer Their Fears.* Black Earth, WI: Dog's Best Friend, Ltd., 1998.

———. *How to Be the Leader of the Pack . . . and Have Your Dog Love You for It!* Black Earth, WI: Dog's Best Friend, Ltd., 1996.

McCullough, Susan. *Housetraining for Dummies.* New York: Howell Book House/Hungry Minds, Inc., 2002.

Miller, Pat. *The Power of Positive Dog Training*. New York: Howell Book House/Hungry Minds, Inc., 2001.

Owens, Paul, with Norma Eckroate. *The Dog Whisperer: A Compassionate Approach to Non-Violent Training*. Holbrook, MA: Adams Media, 1999.

Pryor, Karen. *Clicker Training for Dogs*. Waltham, MA: Sunshine Books, 2001.

Ross, Maureen, and Gary Ross. *Train Your Dog, Change Your Life*. New York: Howell Book House/Hungry Minds, Inc., 2001.

Spector, Morgan. *Clicker Training for Obedience*. Waltham, MA: Sunshine Books, 1999.

Tillman, Peggy. *Clicking with Your Dog: Step-by-Step in Pictures*. Waltham, MA: Sunshine Books, 2001.

Wood, Deborah. *Help for Your Shy Dog*. New York: Howell Book House/Macmillan General Reference, 1999.

———. *The Tao of Bow Wow: Understanding and Training Your Dog the Taoist Way*. New York: Dell Publishing, 1998.

Videos

Bow Wow, Take 2: Clever Tricks and Advanced Skills, Virginia Broitman, 1997.

Clicker Fun series, Deborah Jones (three videos), 1999.

Clicker Magic: The Art of Clicker Training, Karen Pryor, 1997.

Sirius Puppy Training, Ian Dunbar, 1987.

Take a Bow Wow: Easy Tricks Any Dog Can Do, Virginia Broitman and Sheri Lippman, 1996.

Other Resources

Association of Pet Dog Trainers (APDT)
17000 Commerce Parkway, Suite C
Mt. Laurel, NJ 08054
1-800-PET-DOGS (1-800-738-3647)
Fax: 856-439-0525
www.apdt.com
Call the APDT or go to their website to find a list of members in your area. APDT is dedicated to the promotion of positive training, so its members are likely (although not guaranteed) to be positive trainers.

Sound Sensibilities CDs for noise desensitization.
Each CD contains sounds to treat a specific fear (thunderstorms, kitchens, vacuums, fireworks, airport noises, etc.). Each includes a training booklet written by trainer Terry Ryan. Available from:
Hanalei Pets, Inc.
P.O. Box 697
Carlsborg, WA 98324
1-888-876-9364 or 1-360-683-9646 (outside the United States)
Fax: 1-360-683-5755
www.hanaleipets.com

CANINE COMMUNICATION/EVOLUTION

Books

Abrantes, Roger. *Dog Language: An Encyclopedia of Canine Behavior.* Naperville, IL: Wakan Tanka Publishers, 1997.

Clothier, Suzanne. *Body Posture and Emotions: Shifting Shapes, Shifting Minds.* St. Johnsville, New York: Flying Dog Press, 1996.

Coppinger, Raymond, and Lorna Coppinger. *Dogs: A Startling New Understanding of Canine Origin, Behavior and Evolution.* New York: Scribner, 2001.

Coren, Stanley. *How to Speak Dog: Mastering the Art of Dog-Human Communication.* New York: Simon & Schuster, 2000.

Milani, Myrna, D.V.M. *The Body Language and Emotion of Dogs.* New York: William Morrow, 1986.

Rugaas, Turid. *On Talking Terms with Dogs: Calming Signals.* Kula, HI: Legacy by Mail, 1997.

Serpell, James, ed. *The Domestic Dog: Its Evolution, Behaviour and Interactions with People.* Cambridge, UK: Cambridge University Press, 1995.

Video

Calming Signals: What Your Dog Tells You, Turid Rugaas, 2000.

CHOOSING A DOG

Kilcommons, Brian, and Sarah Wilson. *Paws to Consider: Choosing the Right Dog for You and Your Family.* New York: Warner Books, 1999.

Walkowicz, Chris. *Choosing a Dog for Dummies.* New York: Howell Book House/Hungry Minds, Inc., 2001.

Welton, Michele. *Your Purebred Puppy: A Buyer's Guide, Second Edition*. New York: Henry Holt, 2000.

DEATH AND GRIEVING

Kowalski, Gary. *Goodbye, Friend: Healing Wisdom for Anyone Who Has Ever Lost a Pet*. Walpole, NH: Stillpoint Publishing, 1997.

Milani, Myrna. *Preparing for the Loss of Your Pet: Saying Goodbye with Love, Dignity and Peace of Mind*. Rocklin, CA: Prima Publishing, 1998.

Reynolds, Rita M. *Blessing the Bridge: What Animals Teach Us About Death, Dying, and Beyond*. Troutdale, OR: NewSage Press, 2001.

Sife, Wallace. *The Loss of a Pet*. New York: Howell Book House/Macmillan General Reference, 1998.

DIET

Billinghurst, Ian. *The BARF Diet: Raw Feeding for Cats and Dogs Using Evolutionary Principles*. Lithgow, NSW: Ian Billinghurst, 2001.

———. *Give Your Dog a Bone*. Lithgow, NSW: Ian Billinghurst, 1993.

———. *Grow Your Pup with Bones*. Lithgow, NSW: Ian Billinghurst, 1998.

Johnson, Susan K. *Switching to Raw*. Lavon, TX: Birchrun Basics, 2001.

Lonsdale, Tom. *Raw Meaty Bones Promote Health*. South Windsor, NSW: Revetco P/L, 2001.

Martin, Ann. *Foods Pets Die For: Shocking Facts About Pet Food*. Troutdale, OR: NewSage Press, 1997.

McKay, Pat. *Reigning Cats and Dogs, Revised Edition*. Pasadena, CA: Oscar Publications, 1996.

Palika, Liz. *The Consumer's Guide to Dog Food*. New York: Howell Book House/Macmillan General Reference, 1996.

Schultze, Kymythy. *Natural Nutrition for Dogs and Cats: The Ultimate Diet*. Carlsbad, CA: Hay House, 1998.

Segal, Monica. *K9 Kitchen: Your Dog's Diet—The Truth Behind the Hype*. Toronto: Doggie Diner, Inc., 2002.

Strombeck, Donald. *Home-Prepared Dog and Cat Diets: The Healthful Alternative*. Ames, IA: Iowa State University Press, 1999.

Sources for Prepared Raw Food Diets

Aunt Jeni's Homemade 4 Life
P.O. Box 124
Temple Hills, MD 20757
301-702-0123
www.auntjeni.com

Bravo Raw Diet
349 Wetherell Street
Manchester, CT 06040
860-693-0632
www.bravorawdiet.com

Nature's Variety
6200 North 56th Street
P.O. Box 29345
Lincoln, NE 68529
888-519-7387
www.naturesvariety.com

Oma's Pride
Miller Foods, Inc.
308 Arch Road
Avon, CT 06001
1-800-678-6627
www.omaspride.com

Steve's Real Food
Eugene, OR
1-888-526-1900
www.stevesrealfood.com

FLOWER REMEDIES AND OTHER CALMING SUPPLEMENTS

Books

Ball, Stefan, and Judy Howard. *Bach Flower Remedies for Animals.* Essex, UK: The C.W. Daniel Company, 1999.

Callahan, Sharon. *Healing Animals Naturally with Flower Essences and Intuitive Listening.* Mount Shasta, CA: Sacred Spirit Publishing, 2001.

Scott, Martin J., and Gael Mariani. *Dogs Misbehaving: Solving Problem Behaviour with Bach Flower and Other Remedies.* Buckingham, UK: Kenilworth Press, 2001.

Sources for Flower Remedies

Bach flower remedies are available at most health-food stores. Information on Bach flower remedies can be found at www.bachcentre.com.

Anaflora
P.O. Box 1056
Mt. Shasta, CA 96067
530-926-6424
Fax: 530-926-1245
www.anaflora.com

Flower Essence Services (FES)
P.O. Box 1769
Nevada City, CA 95959
1-800-548-0075
Fax: 530-265-6467
www.floweressence.com

Other calming remedies, including l-theanine, for thunderstorm sensitivity:
Pain and Stress Center Products
5282 Medical Drive, #160
San Antonio, TX 78229
210-614-7246 or 1-800-669-2256
www.painstresscenter.com

HEALTH

Goldstein, Martin. *The Nature of Animal Healing: The Definitive Holistic Medicine Guide for Caring for Your Dog and Cat*. New York: Ballantine Books, 2000.

Hamilton, Don. *Homeopathic Care for Dogs and Cats: Small Doses for Small Animals*. Berkeley, CA: North Atlantic Books, 1999.

Kelleher, Donna. *The Last Chance Dog: And Other True Stories of Holistic Animal Healing*. New York: Scribner, 2003.

Pitcairn, Richard, and Susan Hubble Pitcairn. *Dr. Pitcairn's Complete Guide to Natural Health for Dogs and Cats, Revised Edition*. Emmaus, PA: Rodale, 1995.

Puotinen, C. J. *The Encyclopedia of Natural Pet Care*. New Canaan, CT: Keats Publishing, 1998.

———. *Natural Remedies for Dogs and Cats*. Lincolnwood, IL: Keats Publishing, 1999.

Schwartz, Cheryl. *Four Paws, Five Directions: A Guide to Chinese Medicine for Cats and Dogs*. Berkeley, CA: Celestial Arts Publishing, 1996.

———. *Natural Healing for Dogs and Cats A–Z*. Carlsbad, CA: Hay House, 2000.

Volhard, Wendy, and Kerry L. Brown. *Holistic Guide for a Healthy Dog*. Foster City, CA: Howell Book House/IDG Books Worldwide, 2000.

Wulff-Tilford, Mary L., and Gregory L. Tilford. *All You Ever Wanted to Know About Herbs for Pets*. Irvine, CA: Bowtie Press, 1999.

Zucker, Martin. *Veterinarians' Guide to Natural Remedies for Dogs: Safe and Effective Alternative Treatments and Healing Techniques from the Nation's Top Holistic Veterinarians*. New York: Three Rivers Press, 2000.

Video

Your Athletic Dog, Suzanne Clothier, 1995.

Websites

www.alvetmed.com: For information on alternative treatments for a variety of ailments, as well as directories of holistic practitioners.

www.listservice.net/wellpet/index.htm: The website of the long-running wellpet email list provides abundant articles on a variety of pet-related alternative healing topics, many of them gleaned from the list's archives.

Other Resources

To find a holistic vet:
American Holistic Veterinary Medical Association
Dr. Carvel G. Tiekert, Executive Director
2218 Old Emmorton Road
Bel Air, MD 21015
410-569-0795
Fax: 410-569-2346
www.ahvma.org

LEARNING THEORY

Burch, Mary R., and Jon S. Bailey. *How Dogs Learn.* Foster City, CA: Howell Book House/IDG Books Worldwide, 1999.

Pryor, Karen. *Don't Shoot the Dog, Revised Edition.* New York: Bantam Books, 1999.

Reid, Pamela. *Excel-Erated Learning: Explaining in Plain English How Dogs Learn and How Best to Teach Them*. Berkeley, CA: James and Kenneth Publishers, 1996.

LOST DOGS

Sapia, Joseph Andrew, and Patricia Sapia. *The Complete Guide to Lost Pet Prevention and Recovery*. Atlantic Highlands, NJ: Eljebel Press, 2002.

PET-SITTERS

To find a pet-sitter in your area, contact one of these associations:
National Association of Professional Pet Sitters
17000 Commerce Parkway, Suite C
Mt. Laurel, NY 08054
1-800-296-PETS (1-800-296-7387)
Fax: 856-439-0525
www.petsitters.org

Pet Sitters International
201 East King Street
King, NC 27021-9161
336-983-9222
Fax: 336-983-5266
www.petsit.com

TELEPATHIC ANIMAL COMMUNICATION

Adams, Janine. *You Can Talk to Your Animals: Animal Communicators Tell You How*. Foster City, CA: Howell Book House/IDG Books Worldwide, 2000.

Curtis, Anita. *Animal Wisdom: How to Hear the Animals*. New York: iUniverse, 2001.

Fitzpatrick, Sonya, with Patricia Burkhart Smith. *What the Animals Tell Me: Understanding Your Pet's Complex Emotions*. New York: Hyperion, 1997.

Gurney, Carol. *The Language of Animals: 7 Steps to Communicating with Animals*. New York: Dell Books, 2001.

Hiby, Lydia, with Bonnie S. Weintraub. *Conversations with Animals: Cherished Messages and Memories as Told by an Animal Communicator*. Troutdale, OR: NewSage Press, 1998.

Smith, Penelope. *Animal Talk: Interspecies Telepathic Communication, Second Edition*. Hillsboro, OR: Beyond Words Publishing, 1999.

———. *When Animals Speak: Advanced Interspecies Communication, Second Edition*. Hillsboro, OR: Beyond Words Publishing, 1999.

Summers, Patty. *Talking with the Animals*. Charlottesville, VA: Hampton Roads Publishing Company, 1998.

TRAVEL WITH PETS

Books

American Automobile Association. *Traveling with Your Pet: The AAA PetBook*. Orlando, FL: AAA, 2001. (AAA's regular TourBooks also indicate whether hotels accept pets.)

Arden, Andrea. *Fodor's Road Guide USA: Where to Stay with Your Pet*. New York: Fodor's Travel Publications, 2001.

Barish, Eileen. *Vacationing with Your Pet: Eileen's Directory of Pet-Friendly Lodging in the United States and Canada, Fifth Edition*. Scottsdale, AZ: Pet Friendly Publications, 2001.

Grayson, Fred, et al. *The Portable Pets Welcome.Com: The Complete Guide to Traveling with Your Pet*. New York: Howell Book House/Hungry Minds, 2001.

Habgood, Dawn, and Robert Habgood. *On the Road Again with Man's Best Friend (United States)*. Duxbury, MA: Dawbert Press, Inc., 2002. (Regional editions also available.)

Websites

www.freetrip.com: Supplies pet-friendly accommodations on your route.
www.petswelcome.com: Lists pet-friendly hotels, as well as kennels and emergency vets, by state.
www.takeyourpet.com: A low-fee membership-based directory of pet-friendly lodging, with negotiated member discounts, as well as a pet-travel newsletter.

Other Resources

Jiffy Tags (sturdy, temporary tags you can write on) are available from:
Animal Care Equipment and Services, Inc.
P.O. Box 3275
Crestline, CA 92325
1-800-338-ACES (1-800-338-2237)
www.animal-care.com

The Cabana Crate, a collapsible, nylon mesh crate that is great for travel, is manufactured and sold by:
Doggone Good!
320-F Turtle Creek Court
San Jose, CA 95125
1-800-660-2665
www.doggonegood.com

TELLINGTON TTOUCH

Books

Tellington-Jones, Linda. *Getting in TTouch with Your Dog: A Gentle Approach to Influencing Behavior, Health, and Performance.* North Pomfret, VT: Trafalgar Square Publishing, 2001.

Tellington-Jones, Linda, and Sybil Taylor. *The Tellington TTouch: A Revolutionary Natural Method to Train and Care for Your Favorite Animal.* New York: Penguin Books, 1992.

Video

Unleash Your Dog's Potential: Getting in TTouch with Your Canine Friend, Linda Tellington-Jones, 2001.

Website

To learn more about TTouch, see a schedule of seminars, or find a practitioner near you, go to founder Linda Tellington-Jones's website at www.lindatellingtonjones.com.

THE VACCINE CONTROVERSY

McKay, Pat. *Natural Immunity: Why You Should Not Vaccinate.* Pasadena, CA: Oscar Publications, 1997.

O'Driscoll, Catherine. *What Vets Don't Tell You About Vaccines, Second Edition.* Derbyshire, UK: Abbeywood Publishing, 1998.

SOURCES FOR DOG-RELATED BOOKS, VIDEOS, CLICKERS, INTERACTIVE TOYS, AND MORE

www.sitstay.com
www.doggonegood.com
www.dogwise.com

Index

Page numbers in **bold** indicate tables.